Geeks On Call®
Windows® XP

Geeks On Call® Windows® XP

J. R. King

Wiley Publishing, Inc.

Geeks On Call® Windows® XP: 5-Minute Fixes

Published by
Wiley Publishing, Inc.
10475 Crosspoint Boulevard
Indianapolis, IN 46256
www.wiley.com

Published by Wiley Publishing, Inc., Indianapolis, Indiana

Published simultaneously in Canada

ISBN-13: 978-0-471-77456-3
ISBN-10: 0-471-77456-1

Manufactured in the United States of America

10 9 8 7 6 5 4 3 2

1B/TQ/RR/QV/IN

For general information on our other products and services or to obtain technical support, please contact our Customer Care Department within the U.S. at (800) 762-2974, outside the U.S. at (317) 572-3993 or fax (317) 572-4002.

Library of Congress Cataloging-in-Publication Data

King, J. R., 1975–
Geeks on call Windows XP : 5-minute fixes / J. R. King.
p. cm.
Includes index.
ISBN-13: 978-0-471-77456-3 (pbk.)
ISBN-10: 0-471-77456-1 (pbk.)
1. Microsoft Windows (Computer file) 2. Operating systems (Computers) I. Title.
QA76.76.O63K558 2005
005.4'46—dc22

2005026332

Credits

Executive Editor
Carol Long

Development Editor
Tom Dinse

Copy Editor
Kathryn Duggan

Editorial Manager
Mary Beth Wakefield

Production Manager
Tim Tate

Vice President and Executive Group Publisher
Richard Swadley

Vice President and Executive Publisher
Joseph B. Wikert

Project Coordinator
Ryan Steffen

Graphics and Production Specialists
Jennifer Heleine
Lynsey Osborn
Barbara Moore
Alicia B. South

Quality Control Technicians
John Greenough
Brian H. Walls

Proofreading
Sossity R. Smith

Indexing
TECHBOOKS Production Services

Contents

Introduction

The Doctor Will See You Now . . .

In many ways, XP is the most reliable and user-friendly version of Windows to date. However, it is not without problems. If you use XP on a regular basis, you've probably been infected once or twice by Windows Fever—a serious condition marked by elevated blood pressure, sudden verbal outbursts at your computer screen, and the mad desire to toss your entire PC out a window. If you are currently experiencing these symptoms, step away from your computer, count to 10 (better yet, make it 1,000), and swallow two chapters of this book every two hours. If you haven't contracted the disease yet, consider yourself lucky. With a good diet, regular exercise, and the digital preventive medicine found in this book, you can expect to remain free of the fever—at least until the next version of Windows is released.

PART I

TROUBLESHOOT XP

Put Right What Once Went Wrong

During the early 1990s, a popular television program called *Quantum Leap* told the story of a scientist, Sam Beckett, who traveled through time to "put right what once went wrong." Similarly, if parts of Windows XP have gone wrong and no longer work properly, you can put them right by following the 5-minute fixes in Chapters 1 through 4.

1

SOLVE COMMON PROBLEMS

5-Minute Fixes

Although Windows XP is arguably the most stable and reliable version of Windows thus far, it isn't perfect. Occasionally you might hit a few digital potholes that throw XP out of alignment. To ensure a smooth ride and eliminate common XP problems, follow the 5-minute fixes in this chapter.

Do It Yourself

Close an Unresponsive Program

Occasionally, a program may throw the digital equivalent of a temper tantrum and refuse to close. When that happens, you can force it to shut down by using the Task Manager, as follows:

1. Simultaneously press the Ctrl, Alt, and Delete keys on your keyboard, which opens the Windows Task Manager. (However, if your version of Windows is configured differently, then pressing these keys might open a Windows Security box. In that case, simply click the Task Manager button.)
2. Click the Applications tab.
3. Click the name of the unresponsive program.
4. At the bottom of the Task Manager, click the End Task button.
5. If the troubled program doesn't close immediately, a message alerts you that the program is not responding. Click the End Now button.
6. If the program still does not respond, or if Windows feels sluggish, then shut down your computer and restart it.

Delete an Undeletable File

Sometimes files can become corrupt, in which case Windows XP prevents you from deleting them and displays an error message that says the files cannot be deleted because they are currently in use. Even if you reboot your computer and try to delete the files again, usually you see the same error message. To force Windows to delete the files, try the following steps.

To delete common files:

1. Close all open documents and programs that are currently running.
2. Shut down your computer, and then reboot it.
3. Return to Windows and try to delete the file again.
4. If you still can't get rid of the file, shut down your computer.
5. Turn on your computer and immediately press the F8 key on your keyboard several times until the Windows Advanced Options Menu screen appears.
6. Use the up or down arrows on your keyboard to select Safe Mode, and then press the Enter key.
7. The next screen displays the message "Please select the operating system to start." Assuming you have only Windows XP installed on your system, press the Enter key. If you have more than one operating system installed, use the up or down arrows on your keyboard to select Windows XP, then press the Enter key.
8. Windows loads some software, which could take a minute or two. Depending on how your version of Windows is configured, a login screen or the Welcome Screen appears. If you see the login screen, type your account name and password (if you have one), and then press Enter. If you see the Welcome Screen, click the icon for the account labeled Administrator or an account that has administrative privileges, and then type your password (if you have one).
9. A message alerts you that Windows is running in Safe Mode. To proceed, click the Yes button.
10. You can use Safe Mode in much the same way that you use the regular Windows mode. Locate the undeletable file, and then try deleting it again.
11. If you are successful, reboot your computer and return to the regular Windows mode. If your efforts are not successful, seek the help of a certified computer professional like Geeks On Call.

To delete videos with the file extension .avi:

1. Click the Start button in the lower-left corner of Windows.
2. Click the Run button.
3. A window opens. Type **regedit** in the blank, and then click the OK button or press the Enter key.

4. Click the OK button or press the Enter key.
5. The Windows Registry Editor opens. In the left window pane, double-click the registry key labeled HKEY_LOCAL_MACHINE. If you can't find it, do the following:
   a. In the left window pane of the Registry Editor, scroll to the top.
   b. If any of the HKEY registry keys are open—as indicated by a minus sign (-) on their left side—then close them by clicking that minus sign. When a registry key has been properly closed, it will have a plus sign (+) next to it.
   c. Repeat this process for the remaining HKEY registry keys until the only things visible in the left window pane are the five HKEY keys (see Figure 1-1).

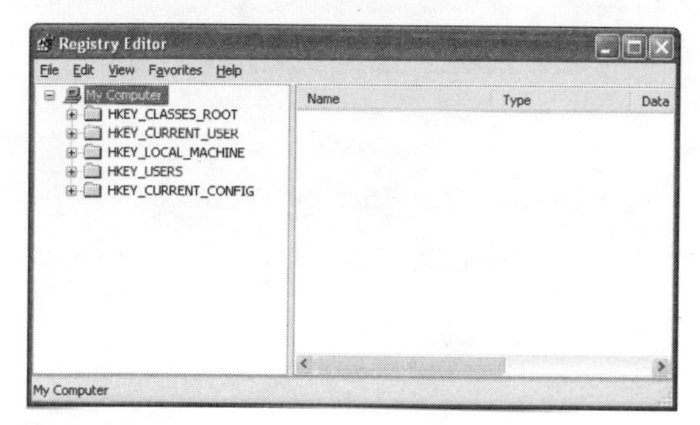

Figure 1-1

Double-click the HKEY_LOCAL_MACHINE registry key.

6. A new column of registry keys appears. Double-click the Software registry key.
7. Open the Classes registry key.
8. A long list of registry keys appears. Scroll down and double-click CLSID (see Figure 1-2).

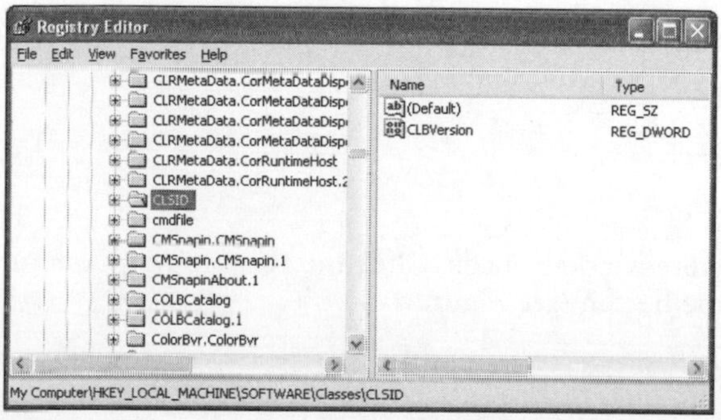

Figure 1-2

9. Another long list of registry keys appears. Scroll down and double-click the one labeled {87D62D94-71B3-4b9a-9489-5FE6850DC73E}.
10. Right-click the InProcServer32registry key, and then select Delete (see Figure 1-3).

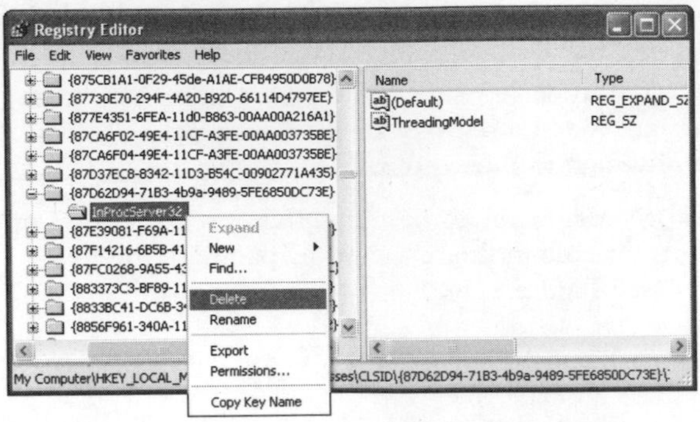

Figure 1-3

11. You are asked to confirm the deletion. Click the Yes button.
12. Exit the Registry Editor by clicking the X button in the upper-right corner.
13. Shut down your computer and restart it.
14. When you return to Windows, you should now be able to delete the .avi file.

Restore Windows to a Healthy State

In a pinch, the Windows XP System Restore feature is a reliable way to recover from a software crisis. In a sense, System Restore sends your computer back in time to a day when it was working properly. If Windows seems like it is undergoing a complete meltdown, try restoring it back to a healthy state, as follows:

1. Click the Start button in the lower-left corner of Windows.
2. Click All Programs.
3. Select Accessories.
4. Select System Tools.
5. Click System Restore.
6. The System Restore window opens. Click the Restore My Computer to an Earlier Time button (see Figure 1-4).

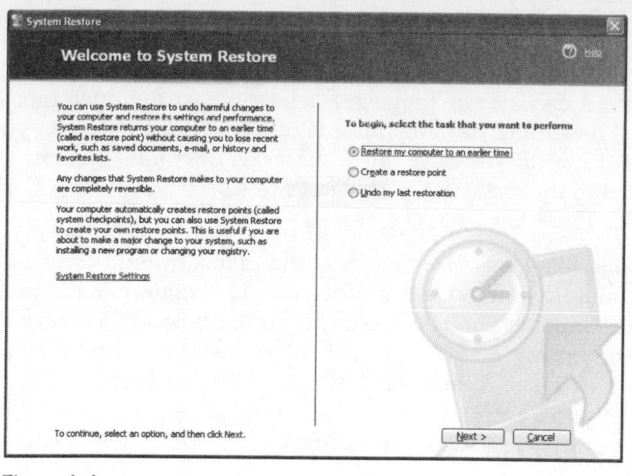

Figure 1-4

7. Click the Next button, located near the lower-right corner of this window.
8. A calendar appears. In it, click on a day when your computer was working properly, then click the Next button .
9. To confirm your choice, click Next.
10. The System Restore process begins. Moments later, your computer automatically restarts itself. When it boots up, follow the on-screen instructions.
11. To make it easier to access System Restore the next time you need it, you can "pin" it to your Start menu (but only if your Start menu is in XP mode rather than classic mode), like this:
    a. Follow Steps 1 through 4 in this procedure to access the System Tools folder.
    b. This time, right-click System Restore and select Pin to Start Menu.
    c. A shortcut to System Restore is placed on your Start menu. From now on, whenever you need to restore your computer to an earlier time, simply click the Start button and then click System Restore.

Use System Restore When Windows Won't Start

When your computer is going haywire, System Restore can be a virtual lifesaver. But what if your high-tech troubles are so severe that Windows can't even start up? In that case, try using the Safe Mode with Command Prompt to access System Restore:

1. After turning on your computer, press the F8 key several times until the Windows Advanced Options Menu screen appears.

2. Use the up or down arrows on your keyboard to select Safe Mode with Command Prompt, and then press Enter.
3. The next screen displays the message, "Please select the operating system to start." Assuming you only have Windows XP installed on your system, press Enter. If you have more than one operating system installed, use the up and down arrow keys to select Windows XP, and then press the Enter key.
4. Windows loads some software, which could take a minute or two. Depending on how your version of Windows is configured, a login screen or the Welcome Screen appears. If you see the login screen, type your account name and password (if you have one), press Enter. If you see the Welcome Screen, click the icon for the account labeled Administrator or an account that has administrative privileges, and then type your password (if you have one).
5. Next, a command prompt appears. Type **%systemroot%\system32\restore\rstrui.exe** in the blank, and then press the Enter key.
6. After several seconds, the System Restore window appears. Click the Restore My Computer to an Earlier Time button.
7. Click the Next button, located near the lower-right corner of this window.
8. A calendar appears. In it, click a day when your computer was working properly, and then click the Next button.
9. To confirm your choice, click Next.
10. The System Restore process begins. Moments later, your computer automatically restarts itself. When it boots up, follow the on-screen instructions.

Protect Windows from a Botched Software Installation

Before you install any new program, you should create a "restore point." Doing so will enable you to undo any problems or damage caused by the software installation. Here's how:

1. Click the Start button in the lower-left corner of Windows.
2. Click All Programs.
3. Select Accessories.
4. Select System Tools.
5. Click System Restore.
6. The System Restore window will open. Click the Create a Restore Point button (see Figure 1-5).

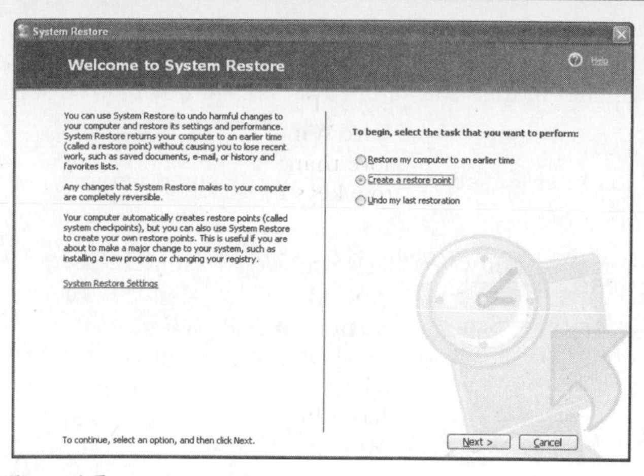

Figure 1-5

7. Click Next.
8. Under the Restore Point Description heading, type some words or sentences that will help you to remember why you are creating this restore point. For example, if you just bought a new antivirus program, you could label this restore point “Before Installation of New Antivirus Software.”
9. Click the Create button.

If a Program Won’t Start or Run Properly

If you suddenly discover that one of your programs will not open or run properly, it could be the result of a software conflict. Occasionally — for some unknown reason — certain programs cannot coexist peacefully on the same computer. In that case, there are some remedies you can try.

Download a Newer Version

Many companies release new versions of their software on a regular basis that offer improved features and resolve problems that were discovered in the previous versions. To update a program:

1. If you can successfully open the troubled program, search for an option with a name like Check for Updates. Usually this can be found in one of the drop-down menus located at the top of the program.
2. If you find this option, you must connect to the Internet so the program can update itself.
3. If you can’t update the program, or if the update doesn’t resolve your problem, check the program manufacturer’s website to see if a newer version is available. If you own a legal copy of the software, you may be able to download the newest version for free.

Download a Patch

Often companies offer small patches that can be downloaded from their websites to fix problems or glitches in their software. To locate and download a software patch:

1. Connect to the Internet and visit the website for the program's manufacturer.
2. Near the top of the website's main page, search for a link with a name like Support or Customer Service.
3. After clicking this link, look for a section labeled Updates or Downloads.

Temporarily Disable Antivirus or Antispyware Software

Although antivirus and antispyware software are essential for the protection and security of your computer, sometimes they can interfere with the actions of other programs. If updating or patching your troubled program doesn't solve its problems, try temporarily disabling or shutting down your antivirus and/or antispyware software. Here's how:

1. If you are connected to the Internet, disconnect from it. For users of dial-up services like AOL, MSN, or Earthlink, this is done simply by logging off your Internet service. For users of high-speed Internet (DSL or cable), this is done by engaging the Internet lock feature of your software firewall or by unplugging the Ethernet cable from the back of your computer.
2. Right-click the icon for your antivirus or antispyware program, which is usually located in the lower-right corner of Windows near the clock.
3. Select the option to Close or Disable or Shut Down.
4. Restart your troubled program to see if it works properly. If it does, then keep your antivirus or antispyware program turned off until you are finished using the troubled program.
5. When you are ready to resume normal computer activities like using e-mail or surfing the Internet, remember to turn on your antivirus software by right-clicking its icon near the Windows clock and selecting Enable or Restore. If the antivirus icon is not there, then you must manually restart the program by doing the following:
   a. Click the Start button in the lower-left corner of Windows.
   b. Click All Programs.
   c. Select the folder containing the name of your antivirus software. For example, if you use Norton AntiVirus, then select the folder labeled Norton AntiVirus.
   d. Click the shortcut to launch the program.

2

ELIMINATE IRRITATIONS

Do certain aspects of Windows XP get under your skin or drive you bonkers? You are not alone. Some of its features have a reputation for causing grown men and women to throw childish temper tantrums or threaten their computers with bodily harm. To soothe these irritations (and keep your blood pressure at a safe level), follow the 5-minute fixes in this chapter.

Prevent Windows Messenger from Loading

The popularity of instant-messaging (IM) software has soared in recent years, prompting Microsoft to join the party. Built into Windows XP is an IM program called Windows Messenger that always seems to hang around even if you never use it. You can correct this by preventing it from loading when Windows starts, as follows:

1. Open Windows Messenger by double-clicking its icon located in the lower-right corner of Windows.
2. Click the Tools drop-down menu.
3. Select Options.
4. A window opens. Click the Preferences tab.
5. Under the General heading, remove the checkmark from the Run Windows Messenger When Windows Starts box. Next, remove the checkmark from the Allow Windows Messenger to Run in the Background box (see Figure 2-1).

Do It Yourself

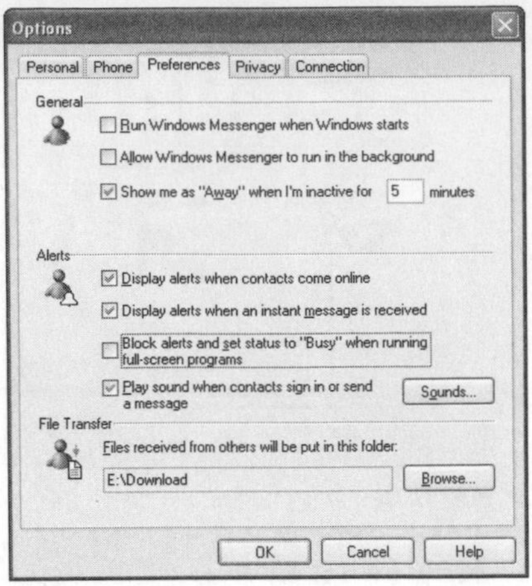

Figure 2-1

6. Click the OK button.
7. Close Windows Messenger, and then open Outlook Express.
8. Click the Tools drop-down menu.
9. Select Options.
10. A window opens. Under the General tab, remove the checkmark from the Automatically Log On to Windows Messenger box.
11. Click the Apply button.
12. Click the OK button.

Hide or Disable Windows Messenger

Even if you tweak Windows Messenger so that it no longer loads when your computer starts, there are still some occasions when it will ignore your wishes and load anyway. To put a stop to Messenger, you need to hide or disable it. There are a few different ways to do this, each of which is equally effective.

Remove Windows Messenger from the Start Menu

This quick fix hides Windows Messenger from sight by removing it from the Start menu. However, no changes are actually made to Messenger, so it remains intact and can be manually located and opened at any time. Follow these steps:

1. Click the Start button in the lower-left corner of Windows.
2. Click the Control Panel. (If you don't see this option, then your Start menu is in classic mode. In that case, click Settings, and then select the Control Panel.)
3. Double-click Add or Remove Programs.
4. A window opens. In the left window pane, click the Add/Remove Windows Components icon.

5. A new window opens. Using the scroll bar on the right, scroll down and locate Windows Messenger. Next to it, remove the checkmark from the box (see Figure 2-2).

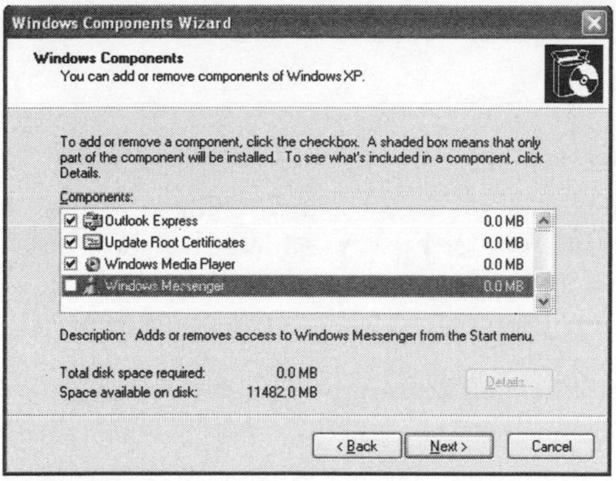

Figure 2-2

6. Click the Next button.
7. Windows begins the process of hiding Messenger from the Start menu, which could take a minute or two. When it has completed, click the Finish button.
8. Exit the Add/Remove window by clicking the X button in the upper-right corner.
9. Although Windows Messenger is now hidden, its shortcut may linger in the lower-right corner of Windows (near the clock). To make this shortcut disappear, right-click it and select Exit.
10. If you change your mind and want to use Windows Messenger again, simply repeat these steps, but this time put a checkmark in the Windows Messenger box.

Rename Windows Messenger's Folder

Another way to get rid of Messenger is to rename its folder, which prevents Windows from locating it. Although this fix is very rudimentary, it successfully stops Messenger from launching. To use this fix, follow these steps:

1. Double-click the My Computer icon on your desktop. If this icon is not available, then click the Start button in the lower-left corner of Windows and click My Computer. If you can't find the My Computer icon anywhere, do the following:
    a. Right-click in the empty space on your desktop.
    b. Select Properties.
    c. A window will open. Click the Desktop tab.
    d. Near the bottom of the window, click the Customize Desktop button.

e. Another window opens. On the General tab, beneath the words Desktop Icons, place a checkmark in the My Computer box.

f. Click the OK button.

g. You will be returned to the previous screen. Click the Apply button.

h. Click the OK button.

i. The My Computer icon appears on your desktop. Double-click it.

2. A window opens. Double-click the icon for your C: drive (unless you installed Windows in a different location, in which case you would double-click that drive letter).
3. Double-click the Program Files folder.
4. Locate the Messenger folder, and then right-click it.
5. Select Rename.
6. Give the folder a name that is easily recognizable, such as MessengerDisabled.
7. If you change your mind and want to use Windows Messenger again, simply rename this folder Messenger.

Force Windows to Use a Different Instant Messenger

Instead of hiding or removing Windows Messenger, you can change the settings in Windows so that it recognizes another program as your default instant messenger. The advantage of this is that it keeps Windows Messenger intact and ready to use whenever you want it.

Note

This option works only on Windows XP computers that have a minimum of Service Pack 1 installed.

To designate a different instant messaging program:

1. Click the Start button in the lower-left corner of Windows.
2. Click the Control Panel. (If you don't see this option, then your Start menu is in classic mode. In that case, click Settings, and then select the Control Panel.)
3. Double-click Add or Remove Programs.
4. A window opens. In the left window pane, click the Set Program Access and Defaults icon.
5. Click the Custom button.
6. Scroll down until you see the Choose a Default Instant Messaging Program heading. Click the Use My Current Instant Messaging

Program button. Next, put a checkmark in the Enable Access to This Program box (see Figure 2-3).

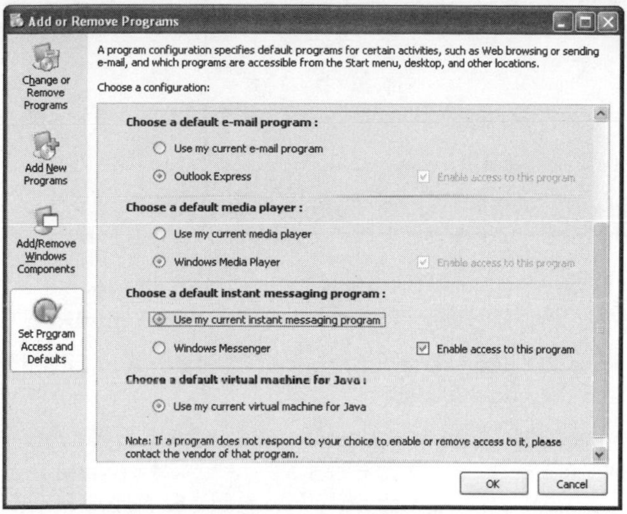

Figure 2-3

7. Click the OK button.

Change the Windows Registration Name

If you bought a previously owned computer, there is a good chance that Windows still says it is registered to its former owner. To remove that name and insert your own, you must edit the Windows Registry:

1. Click the Start button in the lower-left corner of Windows.
2. Click Run.
3. A window will appear. Type **regedit** in the blank, and then click the OK button or press the Enter key.
4. The Windows Registry Editor opens. In the left window pane, double-click the HKEY_LOCAL_MACHINE registry key. If you can't find it, do the following:
   a. In the left window pane of the Registry Editor, scroll to the top.
   b. If any of the HKEY registry keys are open — as indicated by a minus sign (-) on their left side — then close them by clicking that minus sign. When a registry key has been properly closed, it will have a plus sign (+) next to it.
   c. Repeat this process for the remaining HKEY registry keys until the only things visible in the left window pane are the five HKEY keys (see Figure 2-4).
   d. Double-click the HKEY_LOCAL_MACHINE registry key.

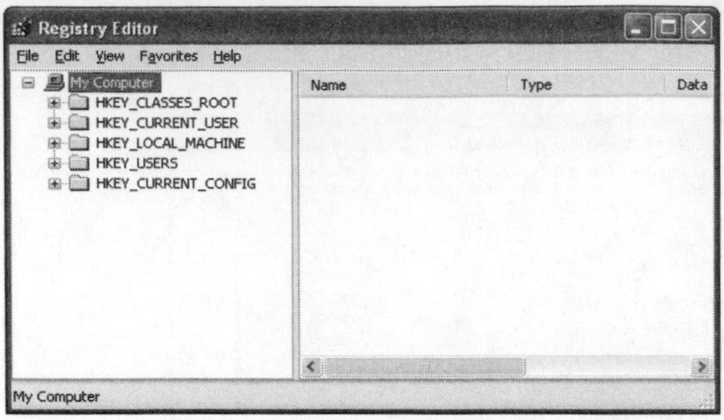

Figure 2-4

5. A new column of registry keys appears. Double-click Software.
6. A long column of registry keys will appear. Scroll down until you find Microsoft, and then double-click it.
7. Another long list of registry keys appears. Scroll down and double-click Windows NT.
8. Click the CurrentVersion registry key.
9. In the right window pane, double-click the RegisteredOwner registry value (see Figure 2-5).

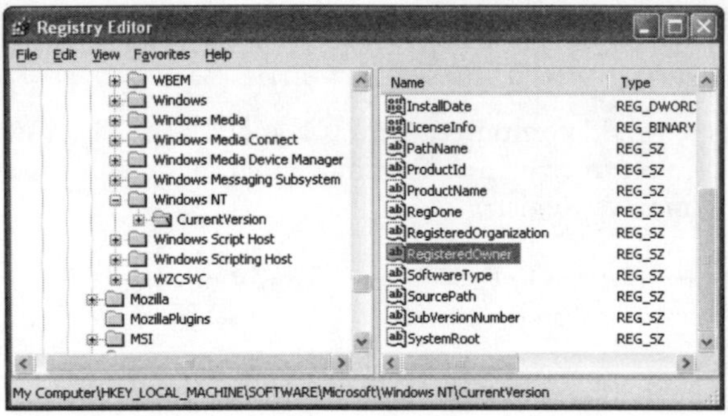

Figure 2-5

10. A window opens. Under the Value Data heading is the name of the previous owner. Delete it, and then type your name in the blank.
11. Click the OK button.
12. Above RegisteredOwner, double-click the registry value named RegisteredOrganization (see Figure 2-6).

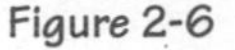

Figure 2-6

13. Under the Value Data heading is the name of the previous owner's employer or organization. Delete it, and then type the name of your organization (or you can just leave it blank if you want).
14. Click the OK button.
15. Exit the Registry Editor by clicking the X button in the upper-right corner.

Pop the Balloon Tips

To make your computer easier to use, Windows XP often displays *balloon tips*, which are advice and hints that pop up for a few seconds, and then disappear. If you prefer not to use balloon tips, you can burst their bubble by disabling them:

1. Click the Start button in the lower-left corner of Windows.
2. Click Run.
3. A window appears. Type **regedit** in the blank, and then click the OK button or press Enter.
4. The Windows Registry Editor will open. In the left window pane, double-click the HKEY_CURRENT_USER registry key. If you can't find it, do the following:
   a. In the left window pane of the Registry Editor, scroll to the top.
   b. If any of the HKEY registry keys are open as indicated by a minus sign (-) on their left side — then close them by clicking that minus sign. When a registry key has been properly closed, it will have a plus sign (+) next to it.
   c. Repeat this process for the remaining HKEY registry keys until the only things visible in the left window pane are the five HKEY keys (see Figure 2-7).
   d. Double-click the HKEY_CURRENT_USER registry key.

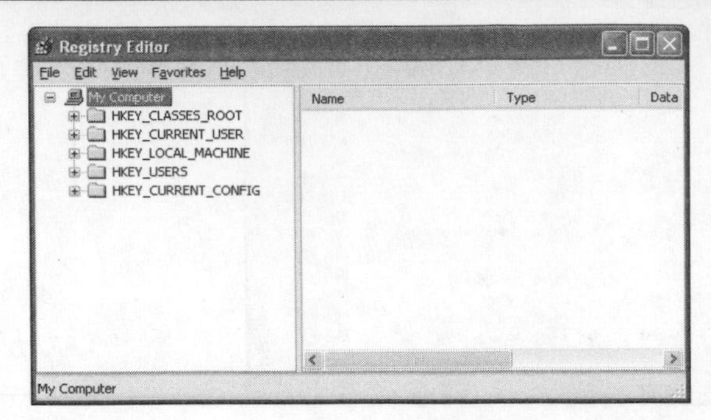

Figure 2-7

5. A new column of registry keys appears. Double-click Software.
6. A long column of registry keys appears. Scroll down until you find Microsoft, and then double-click it.
7. Another long list of registry keys appears. Scroll down and double-click Windows.
8. Double-click the CurrentVersion registry key.
9. Double-click the Explorer registry key.
10. Click the Advanced registry key (see Figure 2-8).

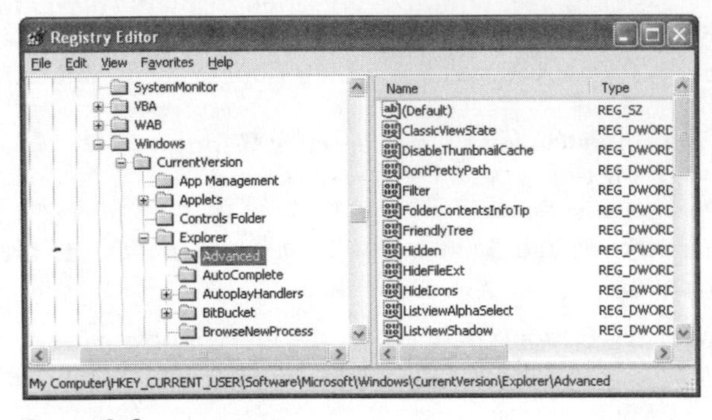

Figure 2-8

11. Click the Edit drop-down menu located in the upper-left corner of the Windows Registry Editor.
12. Select New.
13. Select DWORD Value.
14. In the right window pane, a new registry value appears. Rename it EnableBalloonTips (see Figure 2-9).

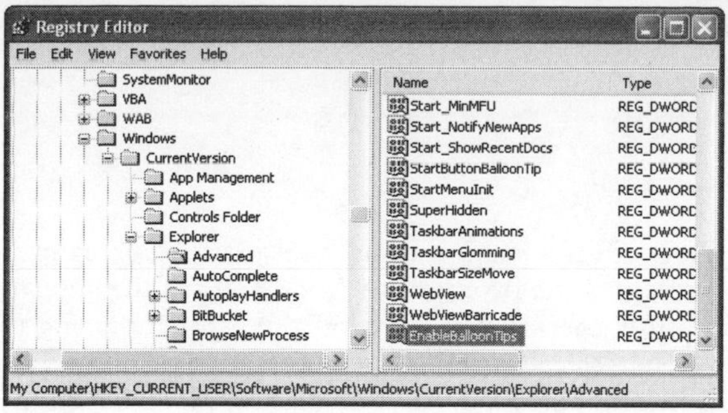

Figure 2-9

15. After renaming the value, double-click it to open it.
16. Under the Value Data heading, make sure there is a 0.
17. Click the OK button.
18. Exit the Registry Editor by clicking the X button in the upper-right corner.
19. If you change your mind and want to allow the balloon tips to appear, all you have to do is repeat these steps to locate the EnableBalloonTips registry key. Open it, delete the 0, and type **1** in its place.

Stop Highlighting New Software

Whenever you install new software, its name will automatically become highlighted in your Start menu's list of programs. The purpose of doing this is to help you quickly find your new software in case you need to configure it. If you find this highlighting to be annoying, you can easily turn it off as follows:

1. Click the Start button in the lower-left corner of Windows.
2. Click the Control Panel. (If you don't see this option, then your Start menu is in classic mode. In that case, click Settings, and then select the Control Panel.)
3. If the Control Panel is in category view, click the Appearance and Themes category, and then click the Taskbar and Start Menu icon. If the Control Panel is in classic view, simply double-click the Taskbar and Start Menu icon.
4. A window opens. Click the Start Menu tab.
5. Click the Customize button.
6. Another window opens. Click the Advanced tab.
7. Under the Start Menu Settings heading, remove the checkmark from the Highlight Newly Installed Programs box.
8. Click the OK button.

9. You are returned to the previous window. Click the Apply button.
10. Click the OK button.

Turn Off Error Reporting

When Windows XP crashes or hits a snag, it usually displays an error message and asks for permission to report the problem to Microsoft via the Internet. To prevent these messages from bothering you, turn off the error-reporting feature:

1. Right-click the My Computer icon on your desktop. If this icon is not available, then click the Start button in the lower-left corner of Windows and right-click My Computer. If you can't find the My Computer icon anywhere, do the following:
    a. Right-click in the empty space on your desktop.
    b. Select Properties.
    c. A window opens. Click the Desktop tab.
    d. Near the bottom of the window, click the Customize Desktop button.
    e. Another window will open. On the General tab, beneath the words Desktop Icons, place a checkmark in the My Computer box.
    f. Click the OK button.
    g. You are returned to the previous screen. Click the Apply button.
    h. Click the OK button.
    i. The My Computer icon appears on your desktop. Double-click it.
2. Select Properties.
3. A window opens. Click the Advanced tab.
4. Click the Error Reporting button located in the lower-right corner of this window.
5. Select the option to Disable Error Reporting. If you still want to be notified when serious errors occur, then put a checkmark in the But Notify Me When Critical Errors Occur box. If you want to disable all types of error reporting so that you never see any error messages, then remove the checkmark from this box.

Disable Step-by-Step Searches

Windows has an internal search companion that enables you to quickly locate files, folders, or programs on your computer. By default, this search engine takes you through a step-by-step process designed to refine your searches and make them more successful. Some computer users prefer to disable this feature to make their searches more streamlined and fast. Here's how:

1. Click the Start button in the lower-left corner of Windows.
2. Click Search.
3. The Windows Search Companion opens. Use the scroll bar to locate Change Preferences, and then click it.
4. Scroll down and click Change Files and Folders Search Behavior.
5. Click the Advanced button.
6. Click the OK button.

Disable the Search Characters

Another aspect of the Search Companion that irritates many people is the animated characters that are supposed to provide entertainment during your searches. If you prefer, you can disable these characters:

1. Click the Start button in the lower-left corner of Windows.
2. Click Search.
3. The Windows Search Companion opens. Use the scroll bar to locate Change Preferences, and then click it.
4. Click the Without an Animated Screen Character option. The character will make a humorous exit and disappear.
5. If you change your mind and want to bring back the animated character, follow the previous steps, but this time click With an Animated Screen Character.

Show Inactive Icons

If you have a large number of programs installed on your computer, you might have noticed that the right corner of Windows is jam-packed with icons that are actually shortcuts to your programs. To keep this area clean, Windows XP automatically hides the icons for any programs that have not been used recently. If you prefer to have these icons remain visible at all times, then you must disable the feature known as Hide Inactive Icons. Here's how:

1. Click the Start button in the lower-left corner of Windows.
2. Click the Control Panel. (If you don't see this option, then your Start menu is in classic mode. In that case, click Settings, and then select the Control Panel.)
3. If the Control Panel is in category view, click the Appearance and Themes category, and then click the Taskbar and Start Menu icon. If the Control Panel is in classic view, simply double-click the Taskbar and Start Menu icon.

4. A window opens. Click the Taskbar tab.
5. Remove the checkmark from the Hide Inactive Icons box.
6. Click the Apply button.
7. Click the OK button.

Re-Sync the Windows Clock

If the clock in the lower-right corner of Windows ever displays the wrong time, you can synchronize it with an atomic clock on the Internet—which will ensure that your computer displays the precise time every time.

Note

This feature is not available on computers that belong to a network "domain" (usually domains are found in offices or other business settings).

To reset your clock:

1. Connect to the Internet.
2. Double-click the clock located in the lower-right corner of Windows. The Date and Time Properties window opens, displaying a clock and a calendar.
3. Click the Internet Time tab.
4. Make sure there is a checkmark in the Automatically Synchronize with an Internet Time Server box. If it is missing, restore the checkmark by clicking the box.
5. Click the Update Now button. Windows attempts to synchronize your clock with an Internet time server. If successful, this results in your computer receiving the accurate time. If it is not successful, then it is possible that it is receiving interference from another program like a software firewall. In that case, do the following:
    a. Temporarily disable your firewall.
    b. Repeat the steps to synchronize your clock.
    c. If this does the trick, then consult your firewall's help menu or contact its manufacturer for assistance in tweaking the firewall to give the Windows clock permission to access the Internet.

Disable Automatic Cleanup of Your Desktop

To keep your desktop free of clutter, Windows XP offers to automatically relocate any shortcuts that haven't been used in quite a while. If you are satisfied with the layout of your desktop and don't want it changed, then you should disable the Desktop Cleanup Wizard, like this:

1. Right-click in the empty space on your desktop.
2. Select Properties.
3. A window opens. Click the Desktop tab.
4. Click the Customize Desktop button located in the lower-left corner.
5. Remove the checkmark from the Run Desktop Cleanup Wizard Every 60 Days box.
6. Click the OK button.

Adjust AutoPlay

When you insert a CD or DVD disc into your computer, the Windows AutoPlay feature springs into action and opens, plays, or displays the files on the disc. To adjust the AutoPlay settings, do the following:

1. Double-click the My Computer icon on your desktop. If this icon is not available, then click the Start button in the lower-left corner of Windows and click My Computer. If you can't find the My Computer icon anywhere, do the following:
    a. Right-click in the empty space on your desktop.
    b. Select Properties.
    c. A window opens. Click the Desktop tab.
    d. Near the bottom of the window, click the Customize Desktop button.
    e. Another window opens. On the General tab, beneath Desktop Icons, place a checkmark in the My Computer box.
    f. Click the OK button.
    g. You will be returned to the previous screen. Click the Apply button.
    h. Click the OK button.
    i. The My Computer icon appears on your desktop. Double-click it.
2. A window opens. Right-click the icon for your CD/DVD burner or other media device.
3. Select Properties.
4. A window opens. Click the AutoPlay tab.
5. You will see a drop-down menu that allows you to choose between seven categories: Music Files, Pictures, Video Files, Mixed Content, Music CD, DVD Movie, and Blank CD (see Figure 2-10). Use this menu to select one of the categories, and then go to the Actions heading below it.

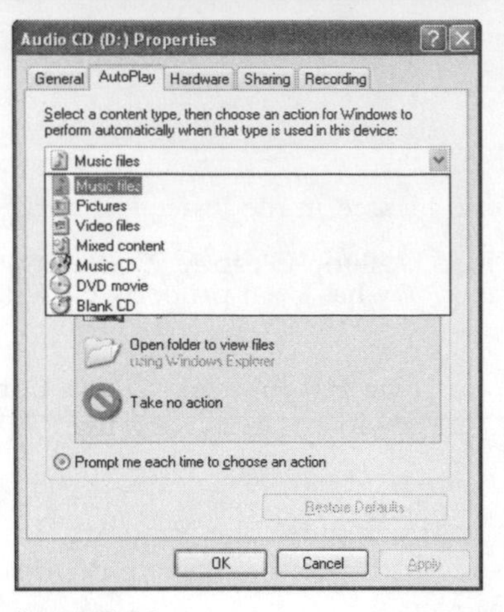

Figure 2-10

6. If you want AutoPlay to ask you what to do each time a disc is inserted into your CD or DVD drive, click the Prompt Me Each Time to Choose an Action button. If you want AutoPlay to automatically perform a specific action each time a disc is inserted, click the Select an Action to Perform button. Next, select one of the options below it. For example, if you want a CD full of digital photos to automatically appear as a slideshow, then do the following:

   a. Click the drop-down menu and select Pictures.

   b. Click Select an Action to Perform.

   c. Click View a Slideshow of the Images.

   There are numerous combinations to choose, so spend time deciding how best to customize AutoPlay to suit your needs.

7. When you are finished configuring AutoPlay, click the Apply button.
8. Click the OK button.

Repair AutoPlay

If AutoPlay isn't working like it should, it might have been turned off accidentally. Follow the steps in the 5-minute fix titled "Disable AutoPlay" to see if any of the AutoPlay categories have been set to Take No Action. If the problem continues, you can fix it by editing the Windows Registry, like this:

1. Click the Start button in the lower-left corner of Windows.
2. Click Run.
3. A window opens. Type **regedit** in the blank, and then click the OK button or press the Enter key.

4. The Windows Registry Editor will open. In the left window pane, double-click the HKEY_LOCAL_MACHINE registry key. If you can't find it, do the following:

   a. In the left window pane of the Registry Editor, scroll to the top.

   b. If any of the HKEY registry keys are open — as indicated by a minus sign (-) on their left side — then close them by clicking that minus sign. When a registry key has been properly closed, it will have a plus sign (+) next to it.

   c. Repeat this process for the remaining HKEY registry keys until the only things visible in the left window pane are the five HKEY keys (see Figure 2-11).

   d. Double-click the HKEY_LOCAL_MACHINE registry key.

Registry Editor
File Edit View Favorites Help
My Computer
HKEY_CLASSES_ROOT
HKEY_CURRENT_USER
HKEY_LOCAL_MACHINE
HKEY_USERS
HKEY_CURRENT_CONFIG
Name Type Data
My Computer

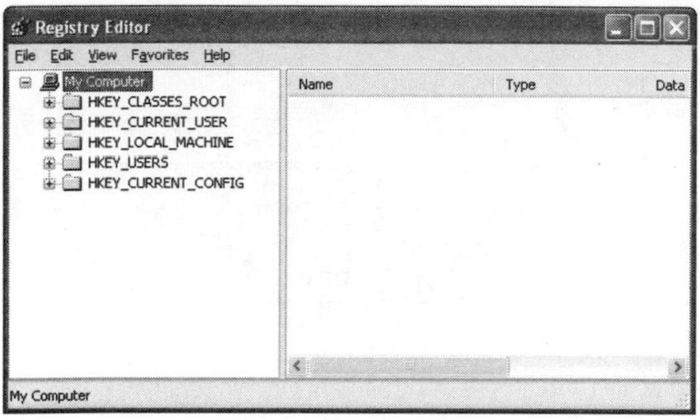

Figure 2-11

5. A new column of registry keys appears. Double-click System.

6. Another column of registry keys appears. Double-click CurrentControlSet.

7. Double-click the Services registry key.

8. A long list of registry keys will appear. Scroll down and click Cdrom (see Figure 2-12).

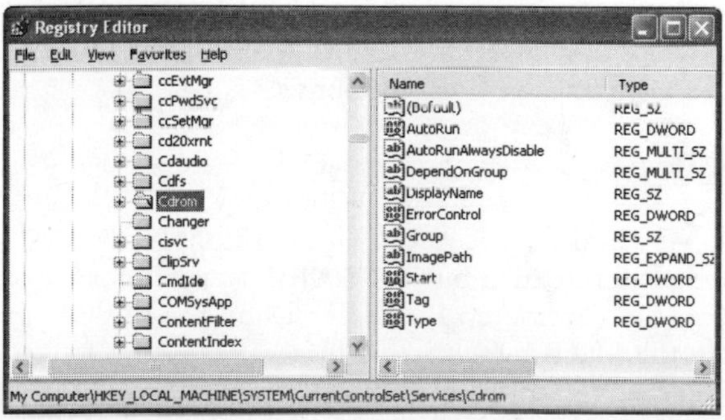

Registry Editor
File Edit View Favorites Help
ccEvtMgr
ccPwdSvc
ccSetMgr
cd20xrnt
Cdaudio
Cdfs
Cdrom
Changer
cisvc
ClipSrv
CmdIde
COMSysApp
ContentFilter
ContentIndex

Name	Type
(Default)	REG_SZ
AutoRun	REG_DWORD
AutoRunAlwaysDisable	REG_MULTI_SZ
DependOnGroup	REG_MULTI_SZ
DisplayName	REG_SZ
ErrorControl	REG_DWORD
Group	REG_SZ
ImagePath	REG_EXPAND_SZ
Start	REG_DWORD
Tag	REG_DWORD
Type	REG_DWORD

My Computer\HKEY_LOCAL_MACHINE\SYSTEM\CurrentControlSet\Services\Cdrom

Figure 2-12

9. In the right window pane, look for a registry value labeled AutoRun (see Figure 2-13). If it is there, then proceed to Step 10. If you do not have this registry value, then you need to create it, like this:

    a. Click the Edit drop-down menu located at the top of the Windows Registry Editor.

    b. Select New.

    c. Select DWORD Value.

    d. In the right window pane, a new registry value will appear. Rename it AutoRun (make sure it looks exactly like Figure 2-13).

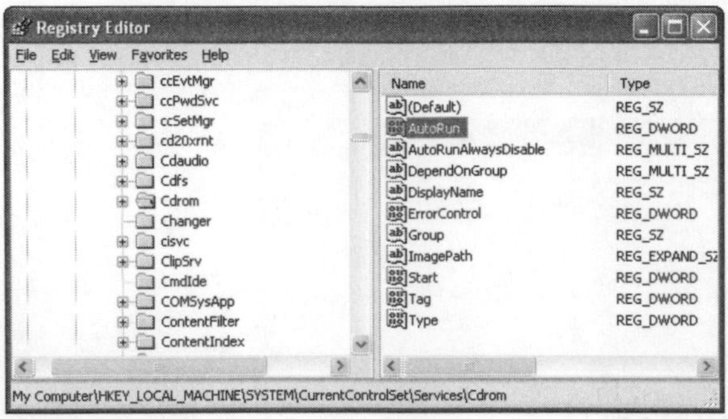

Figure 2-13

10. Double-click the AutoRun value.

11. A window opens. Under the Value Data heading, delete any number you see and type **1** in its place.

12. Click the OK button.

13. Exit the Registry Editor by clicking the X button in the upper-right corner.

Disable AutoPlay

Some people find the AutoPlay feature annoying, and they prefer to have Windows take no action when they insert a disc into their CD or DVD drive. If you want to disable AutoPlay, you have a few options.

For Windows XP Home Edition:

1. Double-click the My Computer icon on your desktop. If this icon is not available, then click the Start button in the lower-left corner of Windows and click My Computer. If you can't find the My Computer icon anywhere, do the following:

a. Right-click in the empty space on your desktop.

b. Select Properties.

c. A window opens. Click the Desktop tab.

d. Near the bottom of the window, click the Customize Desktop button.

e. Another window opens. On the General tab, beneath Desktop Icons, place a checkmark in the My Computer box.

f. Click the OK button.

g. You are returned to the previous screen. Click the Apply button.

h. Click the OK button.

i. The My Computer icon appears on your desktop. Double-click it.

2. A window opens. Right-click the icon for your CD/DVD burner or other media device.
3. Select Properties.
4. A window opens. Click the AutoPlay tab.
5. A drop-down menu appears that allows you to choose between seven categories: Music files, Pictures, Video files, Mixed content, Music CD, DVD movie, and Blank CD. Use this menu to select one of the categories.
6. Under the Actions heading, click the Select an Action to Perform button.
7. Click Take No Action.
8. Repeat this process for each of the seven categories.
9. When you are finished, click the Apply button.
10. Click the OK button.

Alternate Solution: Disable AutoPlay in Windows XP Home Edition

1. Download and install Microsoft's Tweak UI PowerToy. For more information on installing the free PowerToy programs, please see Chapter 8.
2. When the installation is complete, launch Tweak UI.
3. In the left window pane of the Tweak UI interface, double-click My Computer.
4. Double-click AutoPlay.
5. Click Types.

continued

continued

6. In the right window pane, remove the checkmark from the box labeled Enable AutoPlay for CD and DVD drives. Next, remove the checkmark from the box labeled Enable AutoPlay for removable drives as shown in the following figure.

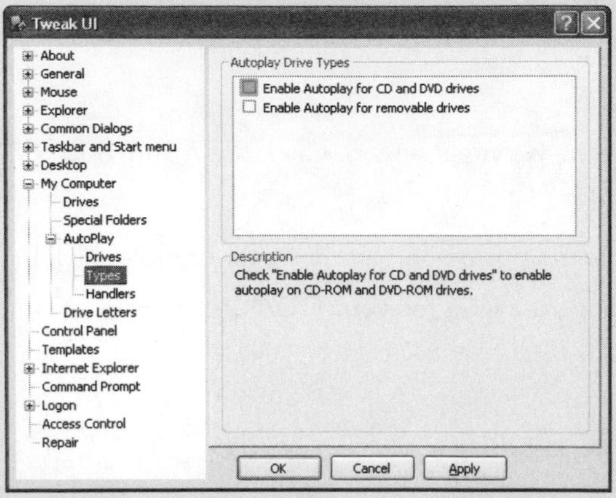

7. Click the Apply button.
8. Click the OK button.

For Windows XP Professional Edition:

1. Click the Start button in the lower-left corner of Windows.
2. Click Run.
3. A window opens. Type **gpedit.msc** in the blank, and then click the OK button or press the Enter key.
4. The Group Policy window will open. In the left window pane, below the words Computer Configuration, double-click the Administrative Templates folder.
5. Single-click the System folder.
6. In the right window pane, double-click Turn Off AutoPlay.
7. Another window opens. Under the Setting tab is a Turn Off AutoPlay heading. Beneath it, click the Enabled button (see Figure 2-14).

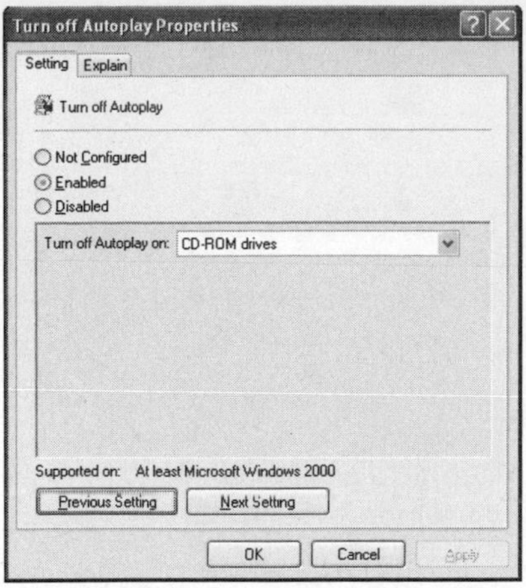

Figure 2-14

8. A drop-down menu appears in the center of the window. Click it, and then choose either to turn off AutoPlay only for the CD-ROM drives or for all drives.
9. Click the Apply button.
10. Click the OK button.
11. Shut down your computer and restart it.

3

5-Minute Fixes

FIX INTERNET ISSUES

One day your Internet is sailing smoothly. The next day it is dead in the water. Sound familiar? From connection difficulties to broken downloads, Internet issues are some of the most common problems that the Geeks On Call technicians fix on a regular basis. Learn the secrets of the pros by following the 5-minute fixes in this chapter.

Do It Yourself

- Repair a broken Internet connection
- Back up your bookmarks
- Restore missing "favicons"
- Prevent crashes when copying text from a website
- Easily locate your downloads
- Prevent broken downloads
- Reduce the Internet cache
- Save QuickTime movies for free
- Block pop-ups

Repair a Broken Internet Connection

Another common problem experienced by Windows XP users is a malfunctioning Internet connection. There are several reasons why this occurs — and just as many remedies.

Temporarily Disable Your Software Firewall

Sometimes a software firewall like ZoneAlarm or Norton Personal Firewall can experience a digital "hiccup" that interferes with the way it monitors and manages your Internet connection. Common symptoms of this problem include a suddenly slow Internet connection, Web pages that stall or are unresponsive, or the complete inability to access the Internet. To determine if your firewall is the cause of your problems, you can temporarily disable it as follows:

1. Right-click the icon for your firewall, which is usually located in the lower-right corner of Windows near the clock.
2. Select the Stop All Internet Activity option (see Figure 3-1).

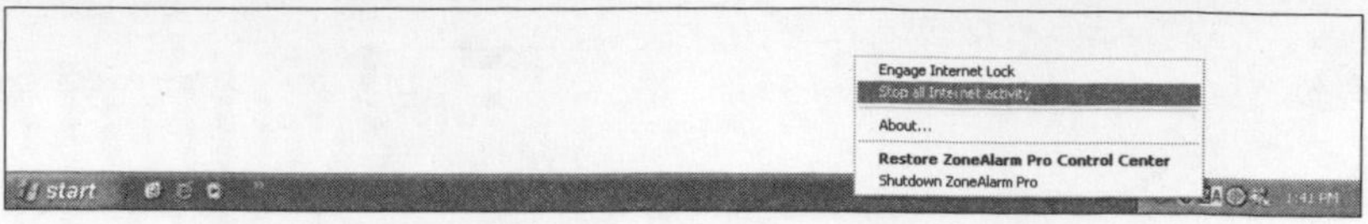

Figure 3-1

3. Try connecting to the Internet. If you are successful, then restart your firewall by right-clicking its icon near the Windows clock and selecting Enable or Restore. If the firewall's icon is not there, then you must manually restart the program by doing the following:
   a. Click the Start button in the lower-left corner of Windows.
   b. Click All Programs.
   c. Select the folder containing the name of your firewall software. For example, if you use ZoneAlarm, then select the Zone Labs folder.
   d. Click the shortcut to launch the program.
4. If re-enabling your firewall causes your Internet connection to malfunction again, then it is likely that your firewall is corrupted and must be reinstalled by following the steps below. This requires its original installation CD-ROM or its digital installer and license key.
   a. Click the Start button in the lower-left corner of Windows.
   b. Click the Control Panel. (If you don't see this option, your Start menu is in classic mode. In that case, click Settings, and then select the Control Panel.)
   c. Double-click Add or Remove Programs.
   d. A window opens. Scroll down the list until you see the name of your firewall.
   e. Click the name of your firewall, and then click the Remove button on its right. If a message pops up and asks you if you want to uninstall the program, click the Yes button.
   f. After the firewall is successfully removed, reinstall it by using its CD-ROM or installer program.

Reboot Your Modem, Your Router, or Both

Sometimes a malfunctioning Internet connection can be caused by an error in computer hardware such as a cable or DSL modem or a router. To correct any problems with these devices, you must reboot them as follows:

1. Shut down your computer.
2. Unplug the power cord from the back of your modem and router. An alternate method is to use the tip of a pencil to push the small reset button located at the rear of the modem or router.

3. The lights on the front of your modem or router go dark. Wait 30 seconds, and then plug the power cord back in. This causes the lights on the front of the modem or router to begin blinking rapidly in a particular pattern. Wait for an additional 30 seconds, and then restart your computer.

Use ipconfig

If temporarily disabling your firewall or rebooting your hardware didn't get you back online, then there might be a problem with your IP address. To resolve this issue, you must use a program called ipconfig. Here's how:

1. Click the Start button in the lower-left corner of Windows.
2. Click Run.
3. A window will open. Type **cmd** in the blank, and then click the OK button or press the Enter key.
4. A command window opens. Type **ipconfig /flushdns** (see Figure 3-2), and then press the Enter key.

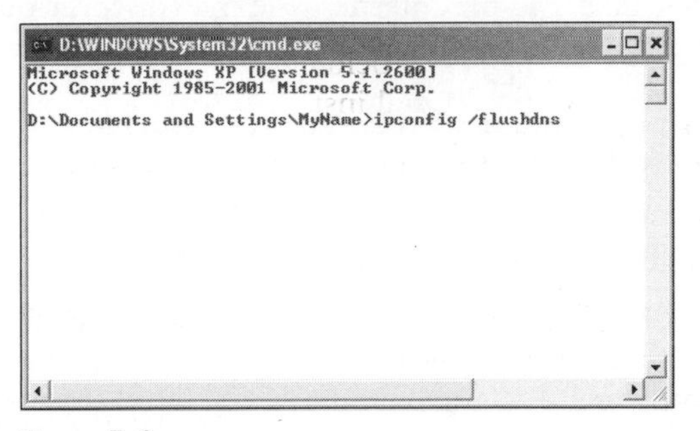

Figure 3-2

5. Type **ipconfig /release** and press the Enter key.
6. Type **ipconfig /renew** and press the Enter key.
7. Close the command window by clicking the X button in the upper-right corner.

Reinstall TCP/IP

On rare occasions, corruption or damage can occur to the section of Windows that handles your Internet connection. To fix this problem, you must reinstall the TCP/IP stack, like this:

1. Click the Start button in the lower-left corner of Windows.
2. Click Run.
3. A window opens. Type **cmd** in the blank, then click the OK button or press the Enter key.

4. A command window opens. Type **netsh int ip reset c:\resetlog.txt** (see Figure 3-3), and then press the Enter key.

Note

If Windows XP is not installed on your C: drive, then you must replace the C: in this command with the correct drive letter followed by 0a colon.

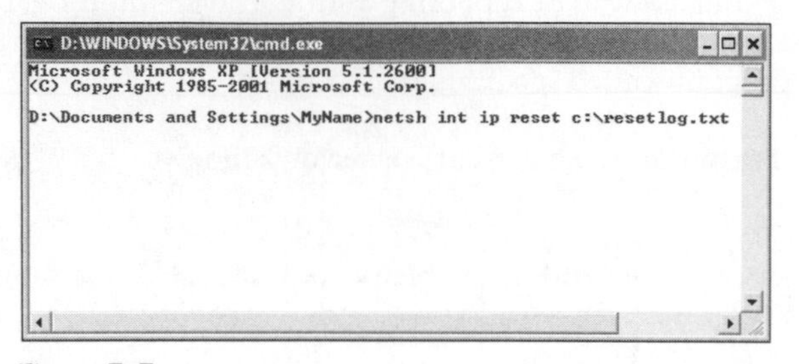

Figure 3-3

5. If you can successfully connect to the Internet, you may discover that this fix has altered or corrupted your antivirus program, antispyware program, software firewall, or other programs that monitor your Internet activity. In that case, you must reinstall those programs by following the steps below. This requires their original installation CD-ROMs or their digital installers and license keys.
   a. Click the Start button in the lower-left corner of Windows.
   b. Click the Control Panel. (If you don't see this option, your Start menu is in classic mode. In that case, click Settings, and then select the Control Panel.)
   c. Double-click Add or Remove Programs.
   d. A window opens. Scroll down the list until you see the name of your antivirus, antispyware, or firewall program.
   e. Click the name of the program, and then click the Remove button on its right.
   f. If a message pops up and asks you if you want to uninstall the program, click the Yes button.
   g. After the software has been successfully removed, reinstall it by using its CD-ROM or its installer program.

Repair the Winsock

Another potential cause of your inability to connect to the Internet is a winsock file that has been altered or damaged by spyware or other digital threats. Fortunately, repairing the winsock is easy to do. The appropriate method of repair depends on whether you have installed a special collection of Windows security patches known as Service Pack 2. Check for it by doing the following:

1. Right-click the My Computer icon on your desktop. If this icon is not available, then click the Start button in the lower-left corner of Windows and right-click My Computer. If you can't find the My Computer icon anywhere, do the following:
   a. Right-click in the empty space on your desktop.
   b. Select Properties.
   c. A window opens. Click the Desktop tab.
   d. Near the bottom of the window, click the Customize Desktop button.
   e. Another window opens. On the General tab, beneath Desktop Icons, place a checkmark next to My Computer.
   f. Click the OK button.
   g. You are returned to the previous screen. Click the Apply button.
   h. Click the OK button.
   i. The My Computer icon appears on your desktop. Double-click it.
2. Select Properties.
3. A window opens. Under the tab labeled General, look for System. Beneath it, you should see some words identifying your version of Windows as well as any service packs that are installed. To repair the winsock, try the fixes in the following sections that correspond to the type of service pack you have (if any).

To repair the winsock if you have no Service Packs or have Service Pack 1:

1. Click the Start button in the lower-left corner of Windows.
2. Click Run.
3. A window opens. Type **regedit** in the blank, and then click the OK button or press the Enter key.
4. The Windows Registry Editor opens. In the left window pane, double-click the HKEY_LOCAL_MACHINE registry key. If you can't find it, do the following:
   a. In the left window pane of the Registry Editor, scroll to the top.
   b. If any of the HKEY registry keys are open—as indicated by a minus sign (-) on their left side—then close them by clicking that minus sign. When a registry key has been properly closed, it will have a plus sign (+) next to it.
   c. Repeat this process for the remaining HKEY registry keys until the only things visible in the left window pane are the five HKEY keys (see Figure 3-4).
   d. Double-click the HKEY_LOCAL_MACHINE registry key.

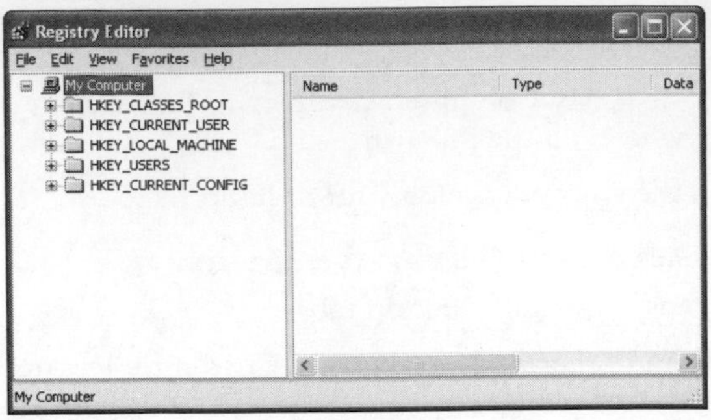

Figure 3-4

5. A new column of registry keys appears. Double-click System.

6. Another column of registry keys appears. Double-click CurrentControlSet.

7. Double-click Services.

8. A long list of registry keys appears. Scroll down until you see Winsock (see Figure 3-5), and then right-click it and select Delete.

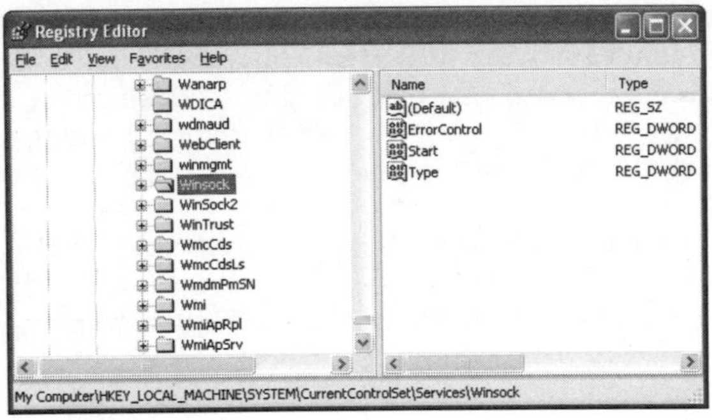

Figure 3-5

9. You are asked to confirm the deletion. Click the Yes button.

10. Repeat this procedure to delete the Winsock2 registry key.

11. Exit the Registry Editor by clicking the X button in the upper-right corner.

12. Shut down your computer and restart it.

13. After returning to Windows, click the Start button in the lower-left corner.

14. Click the Control Panel. (If you don't see this option, your Start menu is in classic mode. In that case, click Settings, and then select the Control Panel.)

15. If the Control Panel is in category view, click the Network and Internet Connections category, and then click the Network Connections icon. If

the Control Panel is in classic view, simply double-click the Network Connections icon.

16. In the right window pane, right-click the name of your network connection.
17. Select Properties.
18. A window opens. Click the Install button (see Figure 3-6).

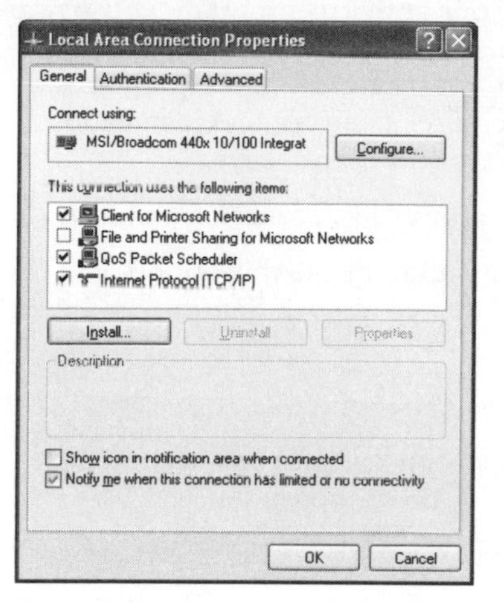

Figure 3-6

19. Another window opens. Click the Protocol icon, and then click the Add button.
20. Under the Network Protocol heading, click Microsoft IPv6 Developer Edition (unless your version of Windows is configured differently, in which case you might see the words Microsoft TCP/IP version 6).
21. Click the Have Disk button.
22. Another window opens. In the box below Copy Manufacturer's Files From, type **C:\Windows\inf** (unless Windows XP is installed in another location, in which case, replace C: with a different drive letter followed by a colon). See Figure 3-7.

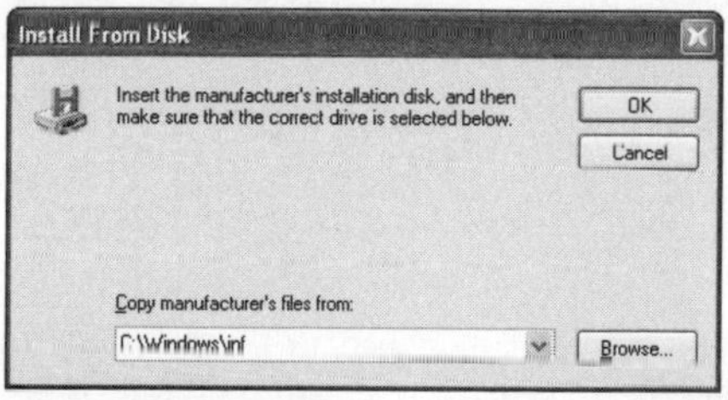

Install From Disk
Insert the manufacturer's installation disk, and then make sure that the correct drive is selected below.
OK
Cancel
Copy manufacturer's files from:
C:\Windows\inf
Browse...

Figure 3-7

23. Click the OK button.

24. A new window opens. Under the Network Protocol heading, click Internet Protocol (TCP/IP), and then click the OK button.
25. A moment later, you are returned to one of the previous windows. Click the Close button.
26. Shut down your computer and restart it.
27. If you can successfully connect to the Internet, you may discover that this fix has altered or corrupted your antivirus program, antispyware program, software firewall, or other programs that monitor your Internet activity. In that case, you must reinstall those programs by following the steps below. This requires their original installation CD-ROMs or their digital installers and license keys.
    a. Click the Start button in the lower-left corner of Windows.
    b. Click the Control Panel. (If you don't see this option, your Start menu is in classic mode. In that case, click Settings, and then select the Control Panel.)
    c. Double-click Add or Remove Programs.
    d. A window opens. Scroll down the list until you see the name of your antivirus, antispyware, or firewall program.
    e. Click the name of the program, and then click the Remove button on its right.
    f. If a message pops up and asks you if you want to uninstall the program, click the Yes button.
    g. After the software has been successfully removed, reinstall it by using its CD-ROM or its installer program.

To repair the winsock if you have Service Pack 2:

1. Click the Start button in the lower-left corner of Windows.
2. Click Run.
3. A window opens. Type **cmd** in the blank, and then click the button labeled OK or press the Enter key.
4. A command window opens. Type **netsh winsock reset** (see Figure 3-8), and then press the Enter key. This restores your winsock to its original, default configuration.

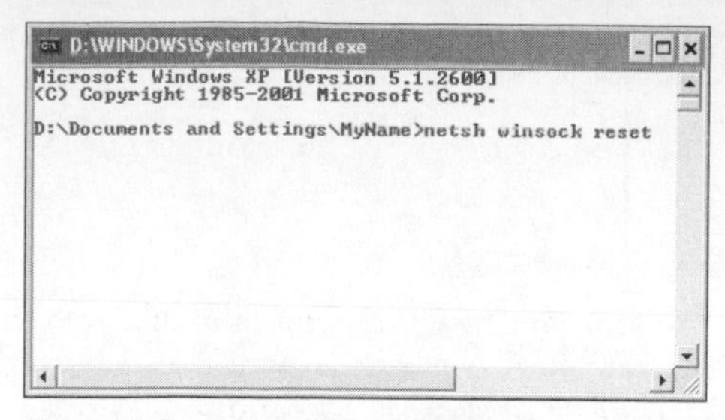

Figure 3-8

5. Shut down your computer and restart it.
6. If you can successfully connect to the Internet, you may discover that this fix has altered or corrupted your antivirus program, antispyware program, software firewall, or other programs that monitor your Internet activity. In that case, you must reinstall those programs by following the steps below. This requires their original installation CD-ROMs or their digital installers and license keys.
   a. Click the Start button in the lower-left corner of Windows.
   b. Click the Control Panel. (If you don't see this option, your Start menu is in classic mode. In that case, click Settings, and then select the Control Panel.)
   c. Double-click Add or Remove Programs.
   d. A window opens. Scroll down the list until you see the name of your antivirus, antispyware, or firewall program.
   e. Click the name of the program, and then click the button on its right labeled Remove.
   f. If a message pops up and asks you if you want to uninstall the program, click the Yes button.
   g. After the software has been successfully removed, reinstall it by using its CD-ROM or its installer program.

Use the System File Checker

Yet another possible cause of your Internet woes is corruption that has occurred in Windows' critical system files. By using a program called System File Checker, you can search for and automatically repair any of these damaged files. Here's how:

1. Click the Start button in the lower-left corner of Windows.
2. Click Run.
3. A window opens. Type **sfc /scanow** in the blank (see Figure 3-9), then click the OK button or press the Enter key.

Figure 3-9

4. Windows scans your computer to determine whether or not your system files are corrupted. If any files need to be replaced, a message may pop up and ask you to insert your Windows XP CD-ROM. Follow the on-screen instructions.
5. If repairs are made, your damaged files may be overwritten by older versions. As a result, some recent security updates and patches may no longer work properly. This could make your computer vulnerable to Internet threats like worms and hackers. To restore your protection, visit the Windows Update website to re-download the patches.

Back Up Your Bookmarks

During your many Internet journeys, you have probably collected countless bookmarks that can whisk you away to your favorite websites with one click of the mouse. If your bookmarks are erased, you'll probably have a difficult time finding your way back to some of those sites, so don't take any chances — back up your bookmarks today. Follow these steps:

1. Open Internet Explorer.
2. Click the File drop-down menu.
3. Select Import and Export.
4. The Import/Export Wizard opens. Click the Next button.
5. Select Export Favorites, and then click the Next button.
6. To export all of your bookmark folders, click the Next button. To export only one folder, click its name, and then click Next.
7. Under the Export to a File or Address heading, click the Browse button.
8. A window opens that allows you to choose the location on your computer where your bookmarks will be saved. Click the Save In drop-down menu, and then select a drive or folder.
9. In the box labeled File Name, type a name for your backed-up bookmarks, such as My Bookmarks or Exported Bookmarks.
10. Click the Save button.
11. You are returned to the previous window. Click the Next button.
12. Click the Finish button.

13. Use a backup device like a CD or DVD burner to save a copy of your exported bookmarks.

Restore Missing "Favicons"

Favicons are the small pictures displayed alongside a website's address (see Figure 3-10). When you create a shortcut to a website — known as a bookmark or a favorite — the favicon for that site is attached to the bookmark. Many computer users enjoy having their bookmarks enhanced by the fun, eye-pleasing favicons and are puzzled when the favicons suddenly vanish. The reason for this disappearance is that favicons are stored in your Temporary Internet Files folder. Whenever this folder is automatically or manually emptied, the favicons are deleted along with all of your old Internet files. Unfortunately, this leaves your bookmarks looking rather bland and lifeless. To correct this problem, you can use a free program called FavOrg that will automatically find and replace your missing favicons, or you can replace them manually.

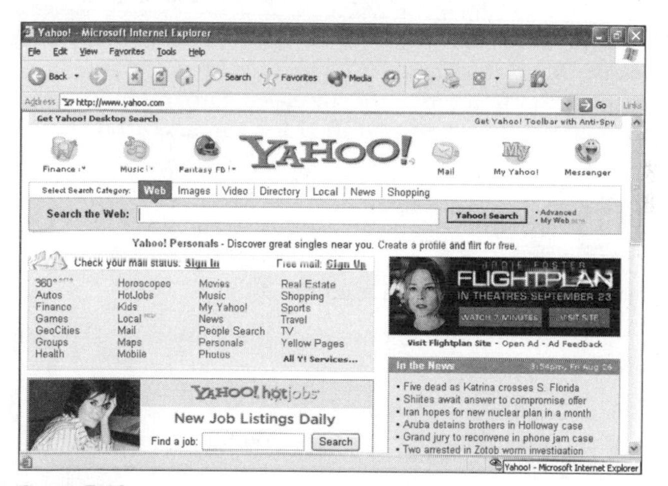

Figure 3-10

Automatically Restore Favicons

There is a wizard, called Extraction Wizard, that you can use to automatically restore your favicons. To use this wizard, follow these steps:

1. Open your Web browser.
2. Go to an Internet search engine like Google (`http://www.google.com`), MSN (`http://www.msn.com`), or Yahoo! (`http://www.yahoo.com`), and search for the word FavOrg.
3. Visit one of the websites offering FavOrg, and then download the program (usually it is packaged in a compressed "zip" file).
4. When the download is complete, right-click the zip file and select Extract All.

5. The Extraction Wizard opens. Click the Next button.
6. If you want to unzip FavOrg in the same folder it was downloaded to, click the Next button. If you want to unzip it in a different folder, click the Browse button, select a new location, and then click the OK button.
7. FavOrg is extracted to your selected folder, which should only take a few seconds. When the process is complete, click the Finish button.
8. Double-click the unzipped FavOrg folder to open it. Inside, double-click the Setup program.
9. The installation of FavOrg begins. Follow the on-screen instructions.

Manually Restore Favicons

If you want to manually select which favicons to restore, follow these steps:

Note

This technique might not work with some websites.

1. Double-click the My Computer icon on your desktop. If this icon is not available, click the Start button in the lower-left corner of Windows and click My Computer. If you can't find the My Computer icon anywhere, do the following:
   a. Right-click in the empty space on your desktop.
   b. Select Properties.
   c. A window opens. Click the Desktop tab.
   d. Near the bottom of the window, click the Customize Desktop button.
   e. Another window opens. On the General tab, beneath Desktop Icons, place a checkmark in the My Computer box.
   f. Click the OK button.
   g. You are returned to the previous screen. Click the Apply button.
   h. Click the OK button.
   i. The My Computer icon appears on your desktop. Double-click it.
2. A window opens. Double-click the icon for your C: drive (unless you have Windows XP installed on a different drive, in which case, double-click the letter for that drive).
3. Click the File drop-down menu located in the upper-left corner.
4. Select New.
5. Select Folder.
6. A new folder appears on your C: drive. Rename this folder Favicons.
7. Open Internet Explorer.

8. In the address bar, type the address of a website that has a favicon you want to capture. For example, type **http://www.yahoo.com** if you want the favicon for Yahoo!
9. After connecting to the website, click the Tools drop-down menu located at the top of Internet Explorer.
10. Select Internet Options.
11. A window opens. Beneath the Temporary Internet Files heading, click the Settings button.
12. Another window opens. Click the View Files button.
13. A Temporary Internet Files folder opens. At the top of this folder, click the View drop-down menu.
14. Select Details.
15. Scroll through the Temporary Internet Files folder and find the favicon that corresponds to the website you just visited (see Figure 3-11).

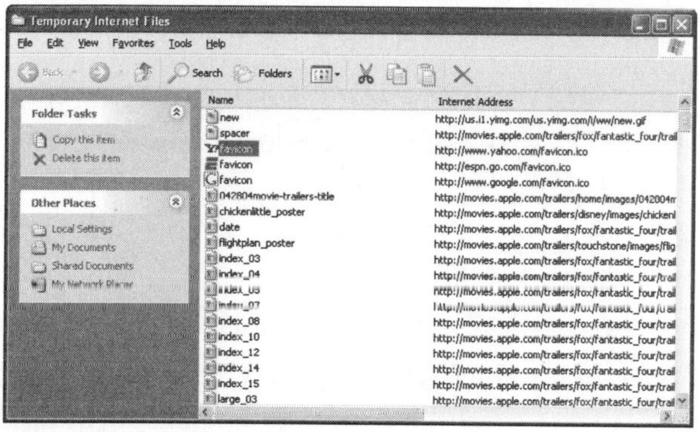

Figure 3-11

16. Right-click the favicon and select Copy.
17. Return to your C: drive.
18. Double-click the Favicons folder you created.
19. Inside this folder, right-click in the empty space and select Paste. This pastes the new favicon into the folder.
20. Return to your C: drive.
21. Double-click the Documents and Settings folder.
22. Double-click the folder containing the name of your Windows account. For example, if your account is named Bob, then click the Bob folder.
23. Double-click the Favorites folder.

24. Locate a bookmark you already have that corresponds to the favicon you just copied. For example, if you copied a favicon for Yahoo!, then locate the bookmark for `http://www.yahoo.com`. If your bookmarks are organized into different folders, you might have to search through them until you find the proper bookmark.
25. Right-click the bookmark and select Properties, which opens the Properties window.
26. Click the Web Document tab.
27. Click the Change Icon button.
28. A new window opens. Click the Browse button that is next to Look for Icons in This File.
29. Another window opens. At the top of it, click the Look in. Next drop-down menu and, select your C: drive.
30. Double-click the Favicons folder.
31. Double-click the favicon you copied.
32. You are returned to the previous window. Click the OK button.
33. You are returned to the Properties window. Click the Apply button.
34. Click the OK button. This creates a permanent link between the bookmark and the favicon.
35. To create lasting favicons for all of your favorite websites, repeat this process as many times as necessary.

Prevent Crashes When Copying Text from a Website

Sometimes when you copy a Web page and try to paste it into Microsoft Word, the graphics in the Web content will cause Word to freeze or crash. To prevent this, try these fixes:

- Do not paste an entire Web page into Word.
- Copy small sections of the Web page and paste them into Word one by one.
- Do not copy text and Web pictures simultaneously.
- If possible, copy and paste each picture or image individually.
- A never-fail alternative is to paste the Web content into Notepad, and then transfer it to Word. This option is ideal for large blocks of text. A word of caution: pasting Web content into Notepad strips out all pictures, images, and graphics, leaving only plain text. If you're okay with that, follow these steps to transfer Web content:
    1. Click the Start button in the lower-left corner of Windows.
    2. Click All Programs.
    3. Select Accessories.

4. Click Notepad.
5. Copy the website text and paste it into Notepad, which will strip the text of its Web format and convert it to plain text.
6. Copy the text from Notepad and paste it into Word.

Easily Locate Your Downloads

Have you ever downloaded a program, video, or picture from the Internet but been unable to find where it went? No matter where you search, you just can't seem to locate it. And because you can't remember the name of the download, the Windows Search Companion is useless. This is a common problem for many Internet surfers. A quick, easy solution is to create a special folder on your hard drive that will store all of your downloads. Here's how:

1. Double-click the My Computer icon on your desktop. If this icon is not available, then click the Start button in the lower-left corner of Windows and click My Computer. If you can't find the My Computer icon anywhere, do the following:
    a. Right-click in the empty space on your desktop.
    b. Select Properties.
    c. A window opens. Click the Desktop tab.
    d. Near the bottom of the window, click the Customize Desktop button.
    e. Another window opens. On the General tab, beneath Desktop Icons, place a checkmark in the My Computer box.
    f. Click the OK button.
    g. You are returned to the previous screen. Click the Apply button.
    h. Click the OK button.
    i. The My Computer icon appears on your desktop. Double-click it.
2. A window opens. Double-click the icon for your C: drive (unless you installed Windows in a different location, in which case, double-click that drive letter).
3. Click the File drop-down menu.
4. Select New.
5. Select Folder.
6. A new folder (aptly named New Folder) appears in your C: drive. Right-click it, and then select Rename.
7. Type a new name for the folder such as Downloads or My Downloads.
8. Each time you download a new file or program, save it to your new downloads folder so that you always know where to find it.

Prevent Broken Downloads

Here is an Internet experience you probably can identify with: your download is nearly complete—97, 98, 99 percent—when suddenly it freezes. Minutes pass, but nothing happens. The download is dead—and now you have to waste time doing it all over again. Fortunately, this frustration is a thing of the past thanks to *download managers*. Not only can these indispensable programs resume a broken download, but they also can speed up the process by dividing the download into small segments that are easier to retrieve. Here are some popular download managers (in no particular order):

- GetRight (`http://www.getright.com`)
- ReGet Pro (`http://pro.reget.com`)

FYI

Stay away from software that claims to boost the speed of your Internet connection. Known as a *Web accelerator, Internet accelerator*, or *Internet optimizer*, this type of program often does more harm than good, and uninstalling it from your computer could actually damage Windows and prevent you from connecting to the Web. If you currently use a slow, dial-up Internet connection and need more speed, the only tried-and-true solution is to sign up for a broadband service like cable or DSL that is offered by your local cable and phone companies.

Reduce the Internet Cache

If you are running out of room on your hard drive, you can free up space by reducing the size of the Internet *cache*, also known as the Temporary Internet Files. This is the place where Internet Explorer stores copies of the images, sounds, and other information related to the websites you have visited recently. The cache actually speeds up your Internet connection by allowing Internet Explorer to view the copies of those Web-related files rather than having to retrieve new versions of them from the Internet. However, this feature can also gobble up precious room on a full hard drive. So if creating extra space is your primary concern, you should reduce the size of the cache. Follow these steps:

1. Open Internet Explorer.
2. Click the Tools drop-down menu.
3. Select Internet Options.
4. A window opens. Under the General tab, look for Temporary Internet Files. Click the Settings button.
5. Another window opens. Find the box with a number in it, which is located next to Amount of Disk Space to Use. This number indicates the size of your Internet cache (listed in megabytes). If you are running seriously low on hard drive space, delete the current number, and in its place type a small number like 50 or 25. If you have a bit more room to spare on your hard drive, you can set the cache at a higher number like 250 or 500.
6. Click the OK button.
7. You are returned to the previous window. Click the OK button.

Save QuickTime Movies for Free

QuickTime is a great program for viewing multimedia content on the Internet, such as the free movie trailers available at `http://www.apple.com/trailers`. However, the basic, free version of this program does not allow you to save videos directly to your desktop. To access that feature, you are required to upgrade to QuickTime Pro (you have to pay for the upgrade). Fortunately, there is a way to get around this problem:

Note

This technique might not work with some QuickTime movies.

1. Open the *free* version of QuickTime. If you have a shortcut to it on your desktop, then double-click it and jump ahead to Step 7.
2. If you cannot find a shortcut to QuickTime, then double-click the My Computer icon on your desktop. If this icon is not available, then click the Start button in the lower-left corner of Windows and click My Computer. If you can't find the My Computer icon anywhere, do the following:
   a. Right-click in the empty space on your desktop.
   b. Select Properties.
   c. A window opens. Click the Desktop tab.
   d. Near the bottom of the window, click the Customize Desktop button.
   e. Another window opens. On the General tab, beneath Desktop Icons, place a checkmark in the My Computer box.
   f. Click the OK button.
   g. You are returned to the previous screen. Click the Apply button.
   h. Click the OK button.
   i. The My Computer icon appears on your desktop. Double-click it.
3. A window opens. Double-click the icon for your C: drive (unless you installed Windows in a different location, in which case, double-click that drive letter).
4. Double-click the Program Files folder.
5. Double-click the QuickTime folder.
6. Double-click the QuickTimePlayer file.
7. QuickTime opens. If a message pops up and suggests that you should upgrade to QuickTime Pro, click the Later button.
8. Click the Edit drop-down menu.
9. Select Preferences.

10. Click QuickTime Preferences.
11. A window opens. Click the drop-down menu and select Browser Plug-in.
12. Put a checkmark in the Save Movies in Disk Cache box (see Figure 3-12).

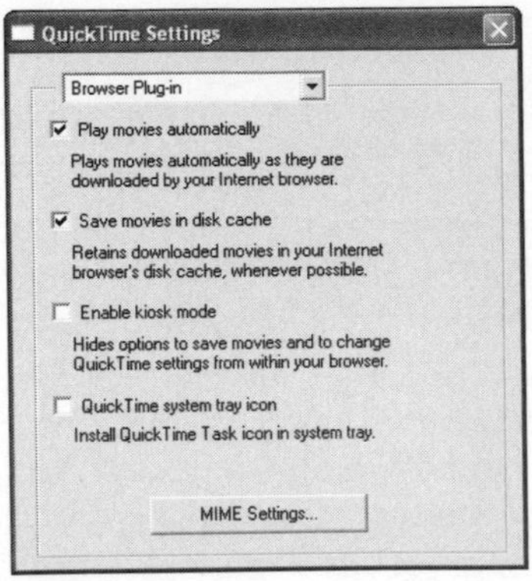

Figure 3-12

13. Exit the window by clicking the X button in the upper-right corner.
14. Connect to the Internet and visit a website like `http://www.apple.com/trailers` that has QuickTime content you want to save to your computer.

Note

Most QuickTime videos have the file extension .mov.

15. View the video in its entirety, and then exit the QuickTime program.
16. To locate a copy of the video you just watched, you need to unhide the Internet cache. Click the Start button in the lower-left corner of Windows.
17. Click the Control Panel. (If you don't see this option, then your Start menu is in classic mode. In that case, click Settings, and then select the Control Panel.)
18. If the Control Panel is in category view, click the Appearance and Themes category, and then click the Folder Options icon. If the Control Panel is in classic view, simply double-click the Folder Options icon.
19. A window opens. Click the View tab.
20. Under the Advanced Settings heading, scroll down and click the Show Hidden Files and Folders button.
21. Click the Apply button.
22. Click the OK button.

23. Double-click the My Computer icon on your desktop. If this icon is not available, then click the Start button in the lower-left corner of Windows and click My Computer. If you can't find the My Computer icon anywhere, do the following:
    a. Right-click in the empty space on your desktop.
    b. Select Properties.
    c. A window opens. Click the Desktop tab.
    d. Near the bottom of the window, click the Customize Desktop button.
    e. Another window opens. On the General tab, beneath Desktop Icons, place a checkmark in the My Computer box.
    f. Click the OK button.
    g. You are returned to the previous screen. Click the Apply button.
    h. Click the OK button.
    i. The My Computer icon appears on your desktop. Double-click it.
24. A window opens. Double-click the icon for your C: drive (unless you installed Windows in a different location, in which case, double-click that drive letter).
25. Double-click the Documents and Settings folder.
26. Double-click the folder that has the same name as your Windows account. For example, if your Windows account is named Bob, then click the Bob folder.
27. Double-click the Local Settings folder.
28. Right-click the Temporary Internet Files folder and select Send To.
29. Click Desktop (Create Shortcut). This creates a desktop shortcut to the cache, which saves you from the hassle of having to manually locate it again in the future.
30. Double-click the Temporary Internet Files folder. This opens the cache.
31. The easiest way to find your QuickTime movie is to sort the files in the cache according to their file type. Click the View drop-down menu.
32. Select Arrange Icons By.
33. Click Type.
34. Use the horizontal scroll bar at the bottom of the cache window to scroll toward the right. Look for the Type column.
35. Use the vertical scroll bar to scroll down the Type column. Look for the QuickTime Movie file-type. This is the video you just watched.

36. Use the horizontal scroll bar to scroll back toward the left. Right-click the name of the QuickTime file and select Copy (see Figure 3-13).

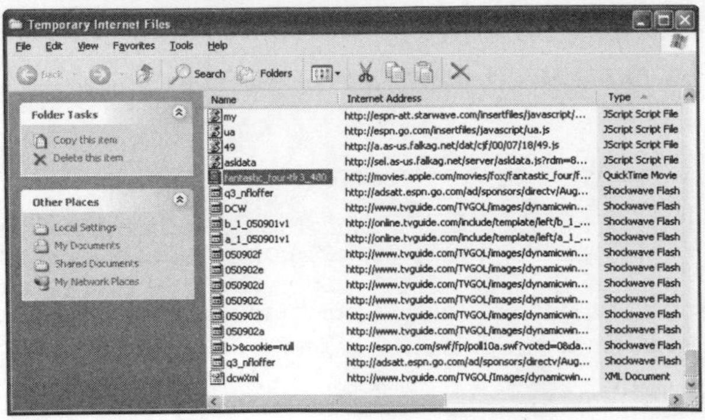

Figure 3-13

37. Exit the cache by clicking the X button in the upper-right corner.

38. Open a folder on your computer where you want to store the QuickTime video (such as the My Documents folder).

39. Inside your chosen folder, right-click the empty space and select Paste. The QuickTime video is pasted into this folder. Now you can play the video normally, just like any other multimedia file on your computer.

40. The final thing to do is re-hide the cache and other special folders.

a. Click the Start button in the lower-left corner of Windows.

b. Click the Control Panel. (If you don't see this option, then your Start menu is in classic mode. In that case, click Settings, and then select the Control Panel.)

c. If the Control Panel is in category view, click the Appearance and Themes category, and then click the Folder Options icon. If the Control Panel is in classic view, simply double-click the Folder Options icon.

d. A window opens. Click the View tab.

e. Under the Advanced Settings heading, scroll down and click the Do Not Show Hidden Files and Folders button.

f. Click the Apply button.

g. Click the OK button.

41. In the future, whenever you want to find another QuickTime video that has been saved to your computer, simply double-click the desktop shortcut you created to the Temporary Internet Files folder. This saves you from the hassle of manually locating the cache all over again.

Block Pop-Ups

Make your Internet experience faster, safer, and less cluttered by using a pop-up blocker to stop annoying Web advertisements from pestering you. This is one of the easiest things you can do to reduce online hassles — and it won't cost you a cent.

There are two types of pop-up blockers:

- **Built-In Blockers**: The latest releases of popular Web browsers like Internet Explorer, Firefox, and Opera have pop-up blockers built into them. If your browser is outdated, this is a great reason to upgrade.

Note

To use Internet Explorer's pop-up blocker, you must install Service Pack 2 from the Windows Update website. For more information on updating Windows, please see Chapter 5.

- **Toolbars**: Several reputable companies offer free toolbars that hook into your Web browser to block pop-ups and provide Internet search capabilities. For example:
  - **Yahoo Toolbar** (`http://toolbar.yahoo.com`); also has an antispyware feature known as Anti-Spy
  - **MSN Toolbar** (`http://toolbar.msn.com`)
  - **Google Toolbar** (`http://toolbar.google.com`)

4

HEAL E-MAIL HEADACHES

If you have used Outlook Express — the e-mail program built into Windows XP — you have probably experienced some stressful, headache-inducing moments while attempting to use or repair its features. In that case, consider the 5-minute fixes in this chapter to be an easy-to-swallow digital aspirin.

Do It Yourself

Back Up E-Mail

How important are the e-mail messages stored on your computer? If they were suddenly wiped out by a hard-drive crash, would your job or personal life suffer? Just like the other files on your computer, your e-mail should be backed up on a regular basis to prevent it from being lost forever. Follow these steps:

1. Open Outlook Express.
2. Click the Tools drop-down menu.
3. Select Options.
4. A window opens. Click the Maintenance tab.
5. Next to Click Store Folder to Change the Location of Your Message Store, click the Store Folder button.
6. A new window opens. Press the Tab key a few times until all of the words are highlighted underneath the Your Personal Message Store Is Located in the Following Folder heading (see Figure 4-1).

Store Location

Your personal message store is located in the following folder:

Change... | OK | Cancel

Figure 4-1

7. Simultaneously press the Ctrl key and the C key, which copies the highlighted text.
8. Click the Start button in the lower-left corner of Windows.
9. Click Run.
10. A window opens. Simultaneously press the Ctrl key and the V key, which pastes the text from Outlook Express.
11. Click the OK button or press the Enter key.
12. A folder opens that contains special dbx files that store your e-mail. Use your backup device—like a CD or DVD burner—to copy these files.

Import E-Mail

If you are switching computers, upgrading to a new computer, or recovering from a hard-drive crash, you can easily import your old e-mail into the new system (assuming you previously backed up those messages). Here's how:

1. If you previously backed up your e-mail folders onto a device like an external hard drive or a rewritable CD/DVD disc, then you must transfer those e-mail folders to your new computer. Be sure to copy them to My Documents or a similar location where they can be quickly and easily found.

Note

You must transfer *all* of your e-mail folders—not just some. Otherwise, Outlook Express gives you an error message when you try to import them.

2. Open Outlook Express.
3. Click the File drop-down menu.
4. Select Import.
5. Select Messages.
6. The Outlook Express Import window opens. Scroll down and click Microsoft Outlook Express 6.
7. Click the Next button.
8. A new window opens. Toward the bottom of it, click the Import Mail from an OE6 Store Directory button.
9. Click the OK button.
10. Click the Browse button, and then select the folder where you just placed your backed-up e-mail folders.

11. Click the OK button, and then click the Next button.
12. In the next window, choose whether to import all e-mail folders or just certain ones. Then, click the Next button.
13. Your messages are imported into Outlook Express. When the process is complete, click the Finish button.

Automatically Spell Check E-Mail

To save yourself the embarrassment of sending an e-mail full of misspelled words, you can configure Outlook Express to automatically spell check your messages before sending them.

1. Open Outlook Express.
2. Click the Tools drop-down menu.
3. Select Options.
4. A window opens. Click the Spelling tab.
5. Under the Settings heading, put a checkmark in the Always Check Spelling Before Sending box.
6. Click the Apply button.
7. Click the OK button.

If Spell Check Is Missing

Unfortunately, Outlook Express doesn't have a built-in spell checker. Instead, it uses the one that comes with Microsoft Office programs like Word and Excel. If you want the ability to spell check your Outlook Express e-mail, you have two options:

- Purchase Microsoft Office software (which can be pricey).
- Download an add-on program that gives you full spell check functionality without spending a fortune. Here are two such programs:
    - **Spellex-Anywhere** (`http://www.spellex.com/products/spxa/default.htm`) can be used for Outlook Express as well as Yahoo mail, Internet forms or forums, and more.
    - **SpellCheckAnywhere** (`http://www.spellcheckanywhere.com`) works with most Windows programs, including Outlook Express and Internet Explorer.

Repair a Malfunctioning Spell Check

Do you have Microsoft Office software installed on your computer but still receive a message like "An error occurred while the spelling was being checked"? Or are you told "The spell check on this document was halted. Do you want to send anyway?" If so, it is possible that a file is corrupt. Here's how to correct the problem:

1. Locate your Windows XP CD-ROM, and then insert it into the CD/DVD drive in your computer.
2. If you have the AutoPlay feature enabled, the CD automatically launches. You should see a window that says "Welcome to Microsoft Windows XP: What do you want to do?" Exit this window by clicking the X button in the upper-right corner.
3. Click the Start button in the lower-left corner of Windows.
4. Click Run.
5. A window opens. In this window, type **expand D:\I386\CSAPI3T1 .DL_ C:\CSAPI3T1.DLL** (see Figure 4-2).

Figure 4-2

Note

This example assumes that Windows is installed on your C: drive, and your CD or DVD drive is installed as the D: drive. If this is not the case with your computer, then simply replace C: with the letter of the drive on which you installed Windows and/or replace D: with the appropriate letter for your CD or DVD drive. For more information on determining what letter your CD or DVD drive has, see the sidebar titled "Determining Your Drive Letter."

6. After typing the command into the window labeled Run, click the OK button or press the Enter key.
7. Windows quickly extracts the file you need and places it on your C: drive. The entire process only takes a few seconds. Next, double-click the My Computer icon on your desktop. If this icon is not available, then click the Start button in the lower-left corner of Windows and click My Computer. If you can't find the My Computer icon anywhere, do the following:
   a. Right-click in the empty space on your desktop.
   b. Select Properties.
   c. A window opens. Click the Desktop tab.

d. Near the bottom of the window, click the Customize Desktop button.

e. Another window opens. On the General tab, beneath Desktop Icons, place a checkmark in the My Computer box.

f. Click the OK button.

g. You will be returned to the previous screen. Click the Apply button.

h. Click the OK button.

i. The My Computer icon appears on your desktop. Double-click it.

8. Double-click the C: icon.
9. In your C: drive, find the csapi3t1.dll file. Right-click this file, and then select Cut.
10. Staying in the C: drive, double-click the Program Files folder.
11. Double-click the Common Files folder.
12. Double-click the Microsoft Shared folder.
13. Double-click the Proof folder.
14. Inside this folder, right-click the empty space and select Paste.
15. You may get a message that says, "This folder already contains a file named 'csapi3t1.dll'—would you like to replace the existing file?" If you see this message, click the Yes button.
16. Shut down your computer and restart it.

Determining Your Drive Letter

It is quick and easy to find out what drive letter your CD or DVD drive has been assigned by Windows XP. Just double-click the My Computer icon on your desktop. If this icon is not available, then click the Start button in the lower-left corner of Windows and click My Computer. A window displays all drives currently on your computer.

If you can't find the My Computer icon anywhere, do the following:

1. Right-click in the empty space on your desktop.
2. Select Properties.
3. A window opens. Click the tab labeled Desktop.
4. Near the bottom of the window, click the button labeled Customize Desktop.
5. Another window opens. On the General tab, beneath the words Desktop Icons, place a checkmark in the box labeled My Computer.
6. Click the OK button.

continued

continued

7. You will be returned to the previous screen. Click the button labeled Apply.
8. Click the OK button.
9. The My Computer icon will appear on your desktop. Double-click it.
10. The My Computer window opens. Find the icon that looks like a compact disc. Next to it or below it is a capital letter enclosed in parentheses. That is the drive letter for your CD or DVD drive.

Back Up the Address Book

When backing up your data, don't forget about your address book, which contains the names, numbers, and addresses of your friends, family, and other contacts. Follow these steps:

1. Open Outlook Express.
2. Click the File drop-down menu.
3. Select Export.
4. Select Address Book.
5. The Address Book Export Tool window opens. Click Text File (Comma Separated Values).
6. Click the Export button.
7. A window opens. Type a name for your address book.
8. Click the Browse button to select the location where you want to save your address book, such as My Documents or another folder where it can be easily located.
9. Click the Next button.
10. You are given the option to select the specific details you want to save in your exported address book, such as the person's full name, e-mail address, phone numbers, and so on (see Figure 4-3). To select a particular detail, put a checkmark in the box next to it. To unselect a detail, remove the checkmark from the box next to it.

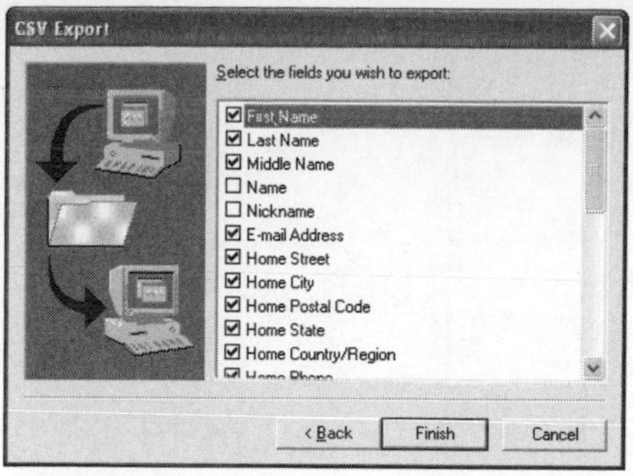

Figure 4-3

11. Click the Finish button. Your address book is saved to the location you previously chose.

Import an Address Book

If you have already backed up your address book, transferring it to a new or different computer is a breeze. Just do this:

1. Open Outlook Express.
2. Click the File drop-down menu.
3. Select Import.
4. Select Other Address Book.
5. The Address Book Import Tool window opens. Click Text File (Comma Separated Value).
6. Click the Import button.
7. Click the Browse button, and then select the folder where your backed-up address book is located (the address book has the file extension .csv).
8. Once you have located the address book, single-click it, and then click the button labeled Open.
9. You are returned to the previous screen. Click the Next button.
10. Under Map the Fields You Wish to Import, select or deselect the contact information you want to import, such as name, address, phone number, e-mail address, and so on (see Figure 4-4). When you are done, click the Finish button.

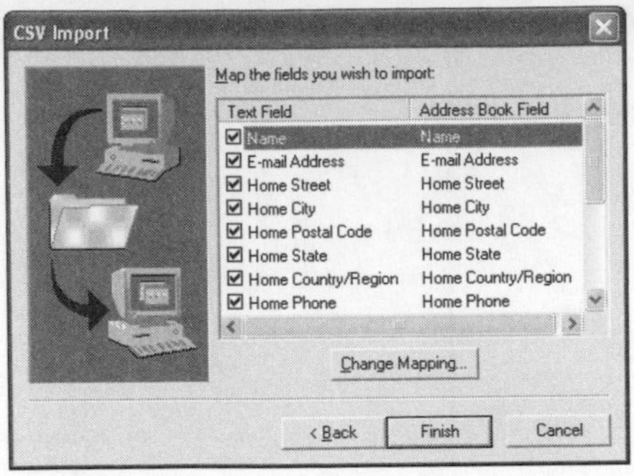

Figure 4-4

11. After a moment or two, you are presented with the message, "Address Book Import Process Has Completed." Click the OK button.

12. You are returned to the Address Book Import Tool. If there are no more address books to import, then click the Close button.

13. To view your restored address book, click the Tools drop-down menu, and then select Address Book.

Change the Location of Your Stored E-Mail

Once in a while, you may find yourself wanting to grab one of the Windows XP designers by the shirt collar and ask, "What the heck were you thinking?" Such is the case with the Outlook Express e-mail folders. For some strange reason, these folders are buried deep within Windows, making it difficult to back them up. To save yourself time and stress, consider changing their location as follows:

1. Choose a drive or folder where you would like to store your e-mail. Pick one that is easy to access and to remember (such as the My Documents folder).

2. To make it even easier to access your e-mail, create a new folder in that location and give it an easily identifiable name.

3. After opening the drive or folder where you want to store your e-mail, click the File drop-down menu located in the upper-left corner of Windows.

4. Select New.

5. Select Folder.

6. A new folder appears. Rename it My E-Mail or something similar that is easy to recognize.

7. Open Outlook Express.

8. Click the Tools drop-down menu.

9. Select Options.

10. A window opens. Click the Maintenance tab.

11. Next to Click Store Folder to Change the Location of your Message Store, click the Store Folder button.
12. A window opens. Click the Change button.
13. Another window opens. In it, browse through the contents of your hard drive until you locate the new e-mail folder you just created in the previous steps.
14. Click the OK button.

Speed Up a Slow Outlook Express

If Outlook Express takes an unusually long time to open, it could be the result of a change made to the instant-messaging program known as Windows Messenger. Because of the link between these two programs, Outlook Express can be affected when Windows Messenger is prevented from launching or is completely disabled. A quick way to fix this problem is to disable the Contacts pane in Outlook Express, like this:

1. Open Outlook Express.
2. Click the View drop-down menu.
3. Select Layout.
4. Under the Basic heading, remove the checkmark from the Contacts box (see Figure 4-5).

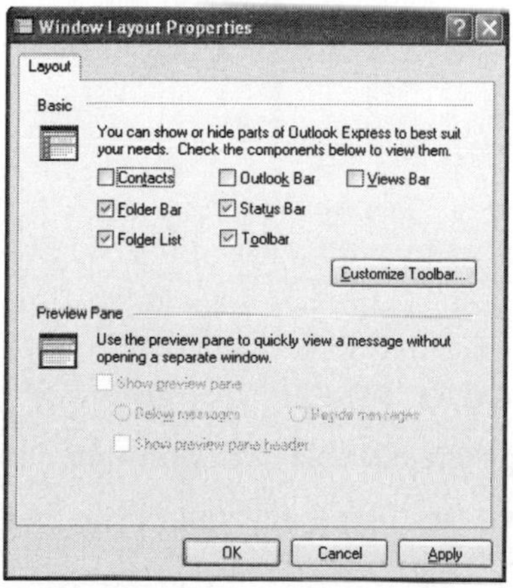

Figure 4-5

5. Click the Apply button.
6. Click the OK button.

Note

If you do not want to disable the Contacts pane, you will have to edit the Windows Registry.

1. Click the Start button in the lower-left corner of Windows.
2. Click Run.
3. A window opens. Type **regedit** in the blank, and then click the OK button or press the Enter key.
4. The Windows Registry Editor opens. In the left window pane, double-click the HKEY_LOCAL_MACHINE registry key. If you can't find it, do the following:
   a. In the left window pane of the Registry Editor, scroll to the top.
   b. If any of the HKEY registry keys are open—as indicated by a minus sign (-) on their left side—then close them by clicking that minus sign. When a registry key has been properly closed, it has a plus sign (+) next to it.
   c. Repeat this process for the remaining HKEY registry keys until the only things visible in the left window pane are the five HKEY keys (see Figure 4-6).

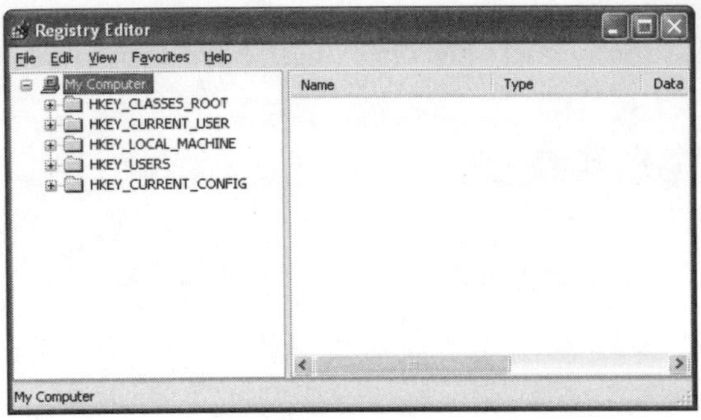

Figure 4-6

   d. Double-click the HKEY_LOCAL_MACHINE registry key.
5. A new column of registry keys appears. Double-click Software.
6. A long column of registry keys appears. Scroll down until you find Microsoft, and then double-click it.
7. Another long list of registry keys appears. Scroll down and single-click Outlook Express (see Figure 4-7).

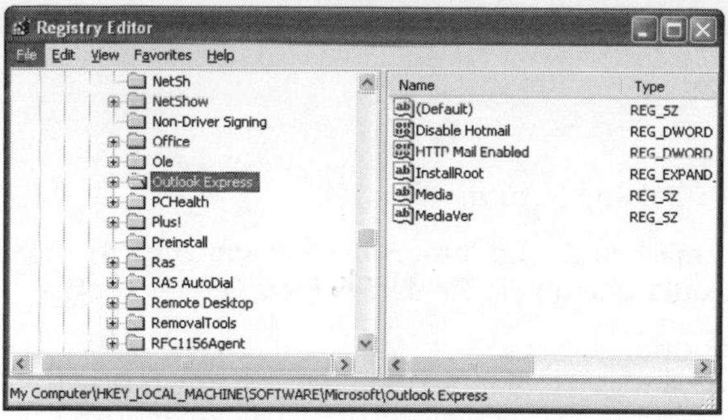

Figure 4-7

8. Click the Edit drop-down menu located in the upper-left corner of the Windows Registry Editor.
9. Select New.
10. Select DWORD Value.
11. In the right window pane, a new registry value appears. Rename it Hide Messenger (see Figure 4-8).

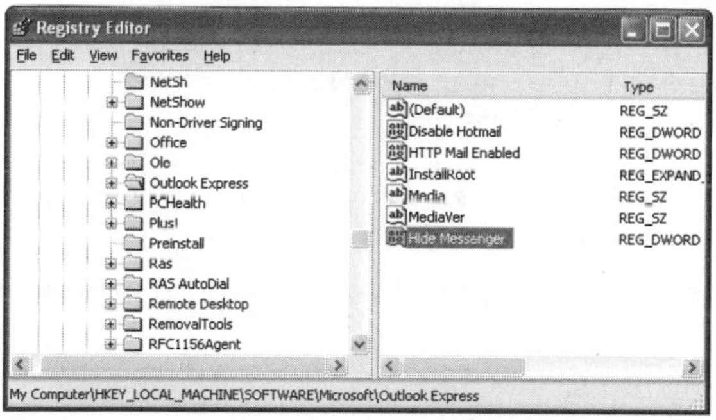

Figure 4-8

12. After renaming the value, double-click it to open it.
13. Under the Value Data heading, type 2 and then click the OK button.
14. Exit the Registry Editor by clicking the X button in the upper-right corner.

View a Blocked E-Mail Attachment

The maximum security settings for Outlook Express automatically block some attachments you receive. This only applies to attachments like executable programs that are widely regarded as carriers of viruses or other digital threats. If you want to receive a blocked attachment, you can temporarily disable this feature:

1. Open Outlook Express.
2. Click the Tools drop-down menu.
3. Select Options.
4. A window opens. Click the Security tab.
5. Remove the checkmark in the Do Not Allow Attachments to Be Saved or Opened that Could Potentially Be a Virus box.
6. Click the Apply button.
7. Click the OK button.
8. When you finish viewing or opening the attachment, return to the Security tab and put back the checkmark in the Do Not Allow Attachments to Be Saved or Opened that Could Potentially Be a Virus box.
9. Click the Apply button.
10. Click the OK button.

View and Print E-Mail Without the ">" Symbol

Often the e-mail you receive is full of annoying "greater than" symbols (>), which can be a nuisance when you are trying to read or print your messages. Here is an easy way to rid yourself of that pesky symbol:

1. Select all of the text inside an e-mail, and then simultaneously press the Ctrl key and the C key.
2. Open a new, blank document inside a word-processing program like Microsoft Word.
3. Paste the text of your e-mail into the new document by simultaneously pressing the Ctrl key and the V key.
4. Use the program's Find and Replace feature to locate all of the > symbols in your text and replace them with a blank space. To do this in Microsoft Word:
    a. Click the Edit drop-down menu.
    b. Select Replace.
    c. A window opens. Type **>** (the "greater than" symbol) in the Find What box.
    d. In the Replace With box, do not type anything (leave it blank), as shown in Figure 4-9.
    e. Click the Replace All button.

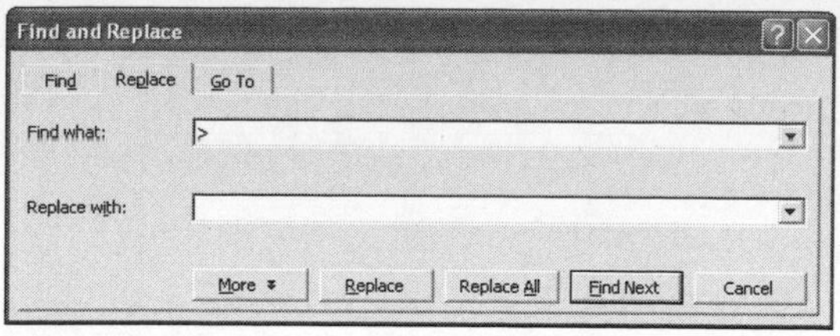

Figure 4-9

Create an E-Mail Shortcut

If you frequently send e-mail to the same contact, here is a great way to save time: create a shortcut on your desktop that instantly opens a new e-mail window and automatically fills in your contact's address.

1. Right-click the empty space on your desktop.
2. Select New.
3. Click Shortcut.
4. The Create Shortcut window opens. In the Type the Location of the Item box, type **mailto:** followed immediately by an e-mail address. For example, mailto:info@geeksoncall.com (see Figure 4-10).

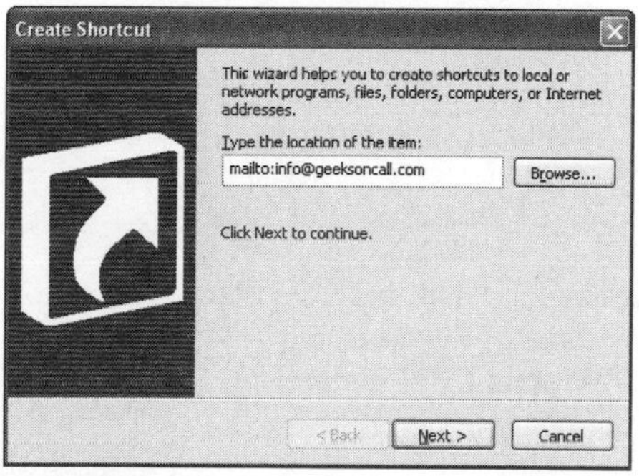

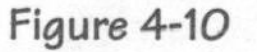

Figure 4-10

5. Click the Next button.
6. In the Type a Name box, type a few words that will help you to identify the shortcut. For example, you could name it E-Mail Shortcut to Geeks On Call.
7. Click the Finish button. The new e-mail shortcut is created on your desktop.
8. Double-click the shortcut to open an e-mail window where you can compose a message.

Remove Wasted Space

A simple way to protect your e-mail folders from being damaged—and to make Outlook Express perform better—is to compact your messages, which will remove any wasted space. Here's how:

1. Open Outlook Express.
2. Click the Tools drop-down menu.
3. Select Options.
4. A window opens. Click the Maintenance tab.
5. Click the Clean Up Now button located on the right side of the window.
6. A new window opens. Look for Wasted Space. Next to this, you will see the amount of wasted space in your e-mail folders. If this amount is greater than five percent, click the Compact button.
7. Outlook Express begins to compact your e-mail, which will remove the wasted space.

Warning
It is critical that you leave your computer alone during this time. Failure to do so could cause your e-mail to become corrupted and inaccessible.

8. When the compacting is complete, click the Close button.
9. Click the OK button.

Prevent E-Mail Corruption

If you send and receive large quantities of e-mail on a regular basis, there are several guidelines you should follow to keep Outlook Express 6 running smoothly and to protect your e-mail folders from becoming corrupt (which could prevent you from accessing them):

- Do not store all of your e-mail in your Inbox. Instead, create new folders, and then move your messages into them.
    1. Open Outlook Express.
    2. Right-click the Inbox folder.
    3. Select New Folder.
    4. A window opens. In the empty box, type a name for your new folder.
    5. Click the OK button. Your new folder is created as a subfolder below your Inbox.
    6. Return to your Inbox, and then drag e-mail messages from it and drop them into your new folder.

- Keep each e-mail folder small. If a folder is stuffed with too many messages, it could become corrupt.
- Do not allow your Sent folder to grow too large. Make a habit of emptying its contents every few weeks.
- Compact your folders at least once a month. For more information, please refer to the "Remove Wasted Space" 5-minute fix in this chapter.
- Install Service Pack 2 for Windows XP, which will improve the way Outlook Express manages and maintains your e-mail.
- Back up your e-mail on a regular basis—particularly if you rely on it for your job. For more information, please refer to the "Back up Your Data" 5-minute fix in Chapter 5.

Recover from E-Mail Corruption

If Outlook Express alerts you that an error has occurred in directdb.dll or msoe.dll, then most likely some or all of your e-mail folders are corrupt. Often this type of corruption is so severe that it prevents Outlook Express from opening. To salvage your e-mail and restore Outlook Express, try the following:

1. Click the Start button in the lower-left corner of Windows.
2. Click Run.
3. A window opens. Type **C:\Documents and Settings*Your Account Name*\Local Settings\Application Data\Identities** as shown in Figure 4-11. (Only part of this command is visible in the figure because of the small window.)

Note

You must replace the words *Your Account Name* with the name of your Windows XP account. For example, if your account is named Bob, then you should type **C:\Documents and Settings\Bob\Local Settings\Application Data\Identities**. Also, if your computer does not have Windows XP installed on the C: drive, then you must insert the appropriate drive letter followed by a colon.

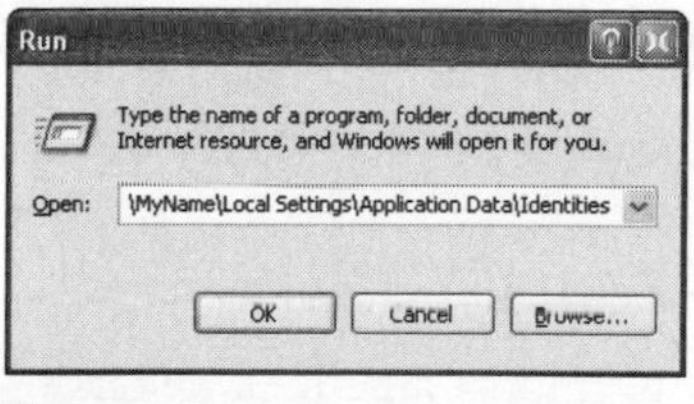

Figure 4-11

4. Click the OK button or press the Enter key.

5. A window opens. Inside, double-click the folder with the strange, long name that looks something like this: {DA1BA02A-D3AE-4E46-A32C-EF70486F8D28}.
6. Double-click the Microsoft folder.
7. Double-click the Outlook Express folder. Inside are all of the special dbx files that store your e-mail. Click the Edit drop-down menu located at the top of this folder.
8. Click Select All. This highlights all of the dbx files.
9. Again, click the Edit drop-down menu.
10. Click Cut.
11. Go to a folder like My Documents, and then create a new folder.
    a. Click the File drop-down menu.
    b. Select New.
    c. Click Folder.
    d. A new folder appears. Rename it something like Outlook Express DBX Files.
    e. Double-click the new folder to open it.
    f. Inside the folder, right-click the empty space and select Paste. All of your dbx files are transferred from their old location to this new one.
12. Try to open Outlook Express. If you are successful, then click the File drop-down menu.
13. Select Import.
14. Click Messages.
15. The Outlook Express Import window opens. Scroll down and click Microsoft Outlook Express 6.
16. Click the Next button.
17. A new window opens. Toward the bottom of it, click the Import Mail from an OE6 Store Directory button.
18. Click the OK button.
19. Click the Browse button, and then locate the folder where you just placed your dbx files.
20. Click the OK button, and then click the Next button.
21. In the next window, choose whether to import all e-mail folders or just certain ones. Then, click the Next button.
22. Your messages are imported into Outlook Express. When the process is complete, click the Finish button.

23. If this process doesn't work — or if some of your e-mail is missing — then you will need to use a special tool named DBXtract to remove each of your e-mail messages from the dbx files. Connect to the Internet and visit `http://www.oehelp.com/DBXtract` to download the program. Follow the on-screen instructions.

PART II

MAKE XP BETTER, STRONGER, AND FASTER

Bionic Makeover

In the mid-1970s, the television shows *The Six Million Dollar Man* and its spin-off *The Bionic Woman* scored big ratings. Their main characters were "cyborgs"—people who had been gravely injured but were saved by medical procedures that replaced their damaged body parts with mechanical "bionic" ones. Doing so enhanced their abilities and made them better, stronger, and faster than normal humans. In a similar way, you can give a bionic makeover to Windows XP that will make it better, stronger, and faster. Just follow the 5-minute fixes in Chapters 5 through 10.

5

AVOID DIGITAL DANGERS

Viruses, spyware, hackers, data loss, or theft — these are just some of the digital dangers your computer faces. Protect your hardware and important files by carefully following the 5-minute security fixes in this chapter.

Manually Update Windows XP

To protect your computer from sinister digital threats like viruses, worms, spyware, and hackers, you must keep Windows updated with the most recent security patches and service packs. If you have not enabled the automatic-update feature of Windows XP, then you will have to download the patches manually. Follow these steps:

1. Connect to the Internet.
2. Open Internet Explorer.
3. In the address box, type: **http://windowsupdate .microsoft.com** (but do not type www in this Web address).
4. After arriving at the Windows Update website, you might be asked to install a small program that will help the site "talk" to your computer. Depending on your version of Windows, click the Yes button or click the Install button. When this process is finished, the main page of the Windows Update site appears.
5. Depending on your version of Windows, click the Express button or the Express Install button (see Figure 5-1).

5-Minute Fixes

Do It Yourself

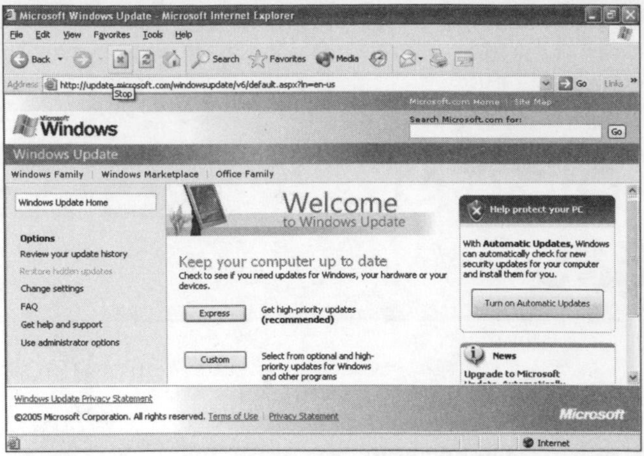

Figure 5-1

6. The Windows Update website scans your computer to determine which security patches are missing. When the scan is finished, follow the on-screen instructions to download and automatically install the updates. It is recommended that you begin by downloading the *service packs*, which are critical collections of various patches and fixes.

Note

Not all security patches, updates, or service packs can be downloaded at the same time. You may need to return to the Windows Update website several times to retrieve all of them.

7. Once the updates are installed, it is likely that you are asked to restart your computer.
8. After your computer reboots, return to the Windows Update website as many times as necessary until all possible security patches and service packs are downloaded and installed.
9. Turn on Windows XP's Automatic Updates feature as explained in the following fix to ensure that you never miss another critical update.

Finding Your Way: Creating Bookmarks for Frequently Visited Web Sites

After connecting to the Windows Update website, create a bookmark (also called a favorite) to make it quick and easy to return to this site. Here's how:

1. If you use Internet Explorer, click the Favorites drop-down menu.
2. Click Add to Favorites.
3. A window opens. In the Name box, give the bookmark a name that makes it easy to identify.

4. Next to Create In, select the folder where you would like to save your bookmark. If you want to create a new folder to put your bookmark in, click the New Folder button, give the folder a name, and then click the OK button.

5. Click the OK button to exit the Favorites window.

Automatically Update Windows XP

To guarantee that your computer is always updated with the most recent Windows security patches, updates, and service packs, turn on automatic updates. Windows XP gives you three options: automatic download/install; download only; and notify only. Here's how to do it:

1. Right-click the My Computer icon on your desktop. If this icon is not available, click the Start button in the lower-left corner of Windows and right-click My Computer. If you can't find the My Computer icon anywhere, do the following:
   a. Right-click in the empty space on your desktop.
   b. Select Properties.
   c. A window opens. Click the Desktop tab.
   d. Near the bottom of the window, click the Customize Desktop button.
   e. Another window opens. On the General tab, beneath Desktop Icons, place a checkmark in the My Computer box.
   f. Click the OK button.
   g. You are returned to the previous screen. Click the Apply button.
   h. Click the OK button.
   i. The My Computer icon appears on your desktop. Right-click it.
2. Select Properties.
3. A window opens. Click the Automatic Updates tab.
4. On the Automatic Updates page, you have a choice (see Figure 5-2):
   - For maximum protection, click the button labeled Automatic (Recommended), which will take care of the updating silently behind the scenes. Use the two drop-down menus to select a day and time for Windows XP to search for updates and install them when necessary.
   - If you would rather have more control over the updates that are installed on your computer, click the button labeled Download updates for me, but let me choose when to install them. Another option is to click the button labeled "Notify me but don't automatically download or install them."

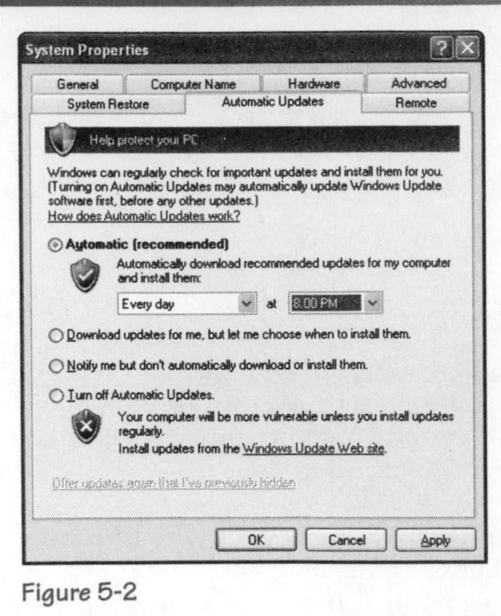

Figure 5-2

5. Click the Apply button.
6. Click the OK button.

Disable Unsafe Services

Windows XP has several Internet features that most home users or home-based businesses will never use. To give your computer an extra measure of protection from digital threats, you can disable some unneeded — and potentially unsafe — services. Follow these steps:

1. Click the Start button in the lower-left corner of Windows.
2. Click the Control Panel. (If you don't see this option, your Start menu is in classic mode. In that case, click Settings, and then select the Control Panel.)
3. If the Control Panel is in category view, click the Performance and Maintenance category, and then click the Administrative Tools icon. If the Control Panel is in classic view, simply double-click the Administrative Tools icon.
4. Double-click the Services icon.
5. A window opens. Using the scroll bar, scroll down until you see Messenger, then double-click it (see Figure 5-3).

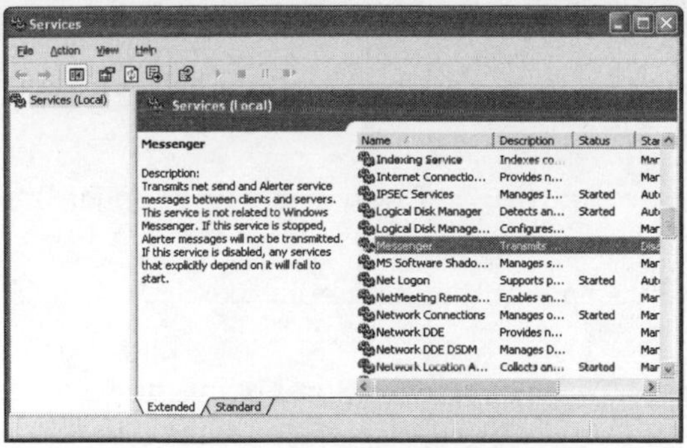

Figure 5-3

6. Another window opens. Click the Startup Type drop-down menu, then select Disabled (see Figure 5-4).

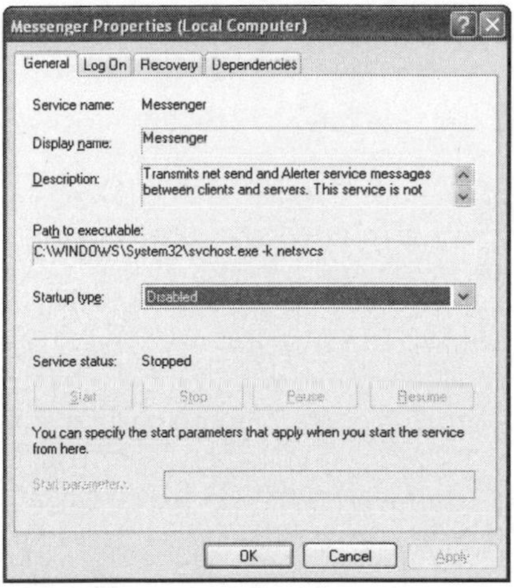

Figure 5-4

7. Click the Apply button.

8. Click the OK button.

9. Return to the Services window, and then repeat the previous steps to disable the following services:

   a. IIS Admin (This service is only available in the Professional Edition of Windows XP)

   b. NetMeeting Remote Desktop Sharing

   c. Remote Desktop Help Session Manager

   d. Remote Registry (This service is only available in the Professional Edition of Windows XP)

   e. Telnet (This service is only available in the Professional Edition of Windows XP)

Protect Your Computer from Viruses

To prevent infection from digital viruses, create some good habits by following all of these tips:

- Install trusted, respected antivirus software and keep it updated constantly.
- Do not open e-mail attachments that have a file extension of .exe, .scr, .vbs, or double file extensions like .txt.vbs.
- Be wary of opening any e-mail attachments or instant-message attachments sent from people you don't know—even if those attachments do not have a dangerous file extension.
- Do not open spam e-mail (selling products, offering free videos, pictures, or songs, and so on).
- Perform a virus scan on files before downloading or opening them.
- Perform a virus scan on e-mail attachments you think are safe to open.
- Do not install pirated software, because often it contains viruses.
- Do not download pirated music files or videos, because they too contain viruses.
- Do not click links sent to you in an instant message.

Antivirus Software

Here are some popular and trusted antivirus programs (in no particular order):

- Norton AntiVirus (`http://www.symantec.com`)
- McAfee Virus Scan (`http://www.mcafee.com`)
- eTrust EZ Antivirus (`http://www.ca.com`)
- PC-cillin (`http://www.trendmicro.com`)
- AVG Anti-Virus (`http://www.grisoft.com`)

Block Worms from Invading Your Computer

Follow these tips to stop Internet worms from sneaking into your computer and causing chaos:

- Most antivirus programs also scan for worms, so install a trusted, respected brand of antivirus software and keep it updated constantly.
- Download the most recent Windows patches, updates, and service packs.

- Turn on the Automatic Update feature of Windows to ensure that it automatically downloads and installs the latest Windows security fixes as soon as they are available.
- Do not open e-mail attachments that have file extensions like .exe, .scr, and .vbs, or have double file extensions like .txt.vbs.
- Be wary of opening e-mail attachments sent from people you don't know.
- Do not click links inside strange e-mails or instant messages (even if the messages are sent from friends or family).
- Do not install pirated software.
- Install the most recent security updates and service packs for all Microsoft Office software (Word, Excel, Access, PowerPoint, Publisher, and so on).

Prevent Spyware Infections

Spyware is a general term describing sinister programs that sneak into your computer by tricking you into installing them or by hiding in other programs you install. The dangers of spyware are that it can do the following:

- Install a "keystroke logging" program that allows a criminal to see everything you type on your keyboard (including passwords and credit-card numbers)
- Hijack your Internet browser and change its default homepage and/or search engine; track your Internet-surfing habits
- Send your private information to hackers who can use it to commit identity theft, or to online marketers who will send you customized pop-up advertisements

How Does Spyware Infect a Computer?

There are numerous ways that spyware can sneak into your computer, including the following:

- **Internet advertisements**: When you click on a malicious pop-up ad, spyware can be downloaded to your computer.
- **File-sharing software**: It hides inside programs used for illegally sharing MP3 music files or pirated movies. When you install the software, the spyware is installed at the same time.
- **Pirated software**: Illegal copies of software purchased on the street or downloaded from the Internet often contain spyware.
- **Shareware and freeware**: It can lurk inside inexpensive or free software available on the Internet from non-reputable vendors or persons.

- **Fake spyware-removal programs**: Believe it or not, some antispyware programs actually install spyware. To stay safe from this scam, only install spyware-removal software that has a solid, respected reputation.
- **E-mail attachments**: Just like a virus, spyware can be installed on your computer when you open an infected e-mail attachment.
- **Hackers**: A hacker who has already found a way into your computer courtesy of a virus, worm, or Trojan horse, can install spyware on your system.

Antispyware Programs

Currently no spyware-removal programs are perfect; all of them catch spyware that the others miss. Your best bet is to install two different programs and use them both to scan for and remove spyware. Antispyware programs fall into two categories: reactive and proactive.

Reactive Antispyware Programs

These programs can remove spyware that already lurks on your computer, but they have little or no capabilities for preventing future infections. Often these programs can be downloaded for free, but give you the option of adding shields by paying a fee or by upgrading to a Pro version.

- Ad-Aware Free Version (`http://www.lavasoftusa.com`)
- Spybot Search and Destroy (`http://www.safer-networking.org`)

Proactive Antispyware Programs

Along with removing spyware, a proactive program can prevent most spyware from sneaking into your computer by placing virtual shields over it. These shields can halt spyware installations, protect your Internet browser's homepage from being hijacked, prevent new bookmarks/favorites from being added to your Internet browser without your permission, block third-party tracking cookies, and much more. These proactive programs must be purchased from an Internet e-merchant or from a brick-and-mortar retail store:

> **It's a Fact**
>
> Approximately 90 percent of all computers worldwide that use the Internet have been — or currently are — infected with spyware.

- Spy Sweeper (`http://www.webroot.com`)
- eTrust PestPatrol (`http://www.ca.com`)
- McAfee AntiSpyware (`http://www.mcafee.com`)

Beware of Phishing Scams

Phishing (pronounced "fishing") is a scam that tricks people into revealing their private, personal information (like credit-card numbers and passwords). Originally, phishing was an e-mail scam in which criminals sent a fake "urgent" message that appeared to be from a respected company or financial institution. The message asked its recipients to verify or update their account information by clicking a link in the e-mail and visiting a special website. When the victims followed the instructions, the information they entered on the fake website was captured by the criminals and used to commit identity theft. In recent years, this crime has produced several sinister spin-offs. Now, phishing is used more as a term to refer to data-mining scams in general.

Here are some tips to avoid phishing:

- **Don't respond to e-mail asking for private information**: Instead, be proactive and call the bank or company and ask them whether they are trying to get in touch with you. Most financial institutions have toll-free phone numbers you can call (usually the numbers are listed on the back of your credit cards).
- **Don't click on links in strange or unexpected e-mail**: This is especially true of those that appear to be from financial institutions.
- **Read your e-mail offline (disconnected from the Internet)**: This will prevent hostile code from being downloaded to your computer if you accidentally click a phishing link in an e-mail. For dial-up users, this is easy: simply log-off your Internet service. For users of always-on, high-speed cable/DSL connections, you will need to turn on the "lock" feature of your software firewall to halt all inbound and outbound Internet activity.
- **Don't click links inside Instant Messages**: This is true regardless of whether or not the link was sent to you from someone on your "buddy" list of contacts.
- **Never send your personal or financial information in an e-mail or instant message**: Like credit-card numbers, social-security numbers, bank-account numbers, passwords, user names, and so on. A normal e-mail or instant message does not have encryption protection, which means it could be intercepted by a criminal who could use your private information to commit identity theft. If you need to give important information to someone, call him or her on the telephone — but only use a landline, because cell-phone calls can also be intercepted.
- **Beware of telephone phishing**: Do not respond to voicemails from companies asking you to call a special phone number to clear up information about your account. This could be phone phishing. Instead, call their central phone number and find out whether or not they really need to speak with you. Also, be suspicious of companies who call you out of the blue and ask you to verify information like

your account number, password, PIN number, mother's maiden name, social-security number, age, home address, and so on. Don't tell them anything. Instead, hang up and call their central phone number.

- **Install an anti-phishing toolbar**: A few companies offer free software toolbars that can be added to your Internet browser to protect you from accidentally visiting phishing websites. Here are a few:
  - Netcraft Toolbar (`http://toolbar.netcraft.com`)
  - TrustWatch Toolbar (`http://www.trustwatch.com`)
  - Cloudmark SafetyBar (`http://www.cloudmark.com`)

Control Cookies

Computer cookies are small text files that store information about the websites you have visited and the things you did on those sites. Cookies come in two flavors: trustworthy—which assist and support your Internet usage—and tracking—which are used by Internet marketers to show you customized advertisements. To control the cookies that are placed on your computer, do the following:

1. Open Internet Explorer.
2. Click the Tools drop-down menu.
3. Select Internet Options.
4. A window opens. Click the Privacy tab.
5. Click the Advanced button.
6. Put a checkmark in the Override Automatic Cookie Handling box.
7. Under the First-party Cookies heading, click the Block button.
8. Put a checkmark in the Always Allow Session Cookies box. This allows websites to place a cookie on your computer that expires the moment you exit the site (which means the cookie cannot be used to track you).
9. Under the Third-party Cookies heading, click the Block button (see Figure 5-5).

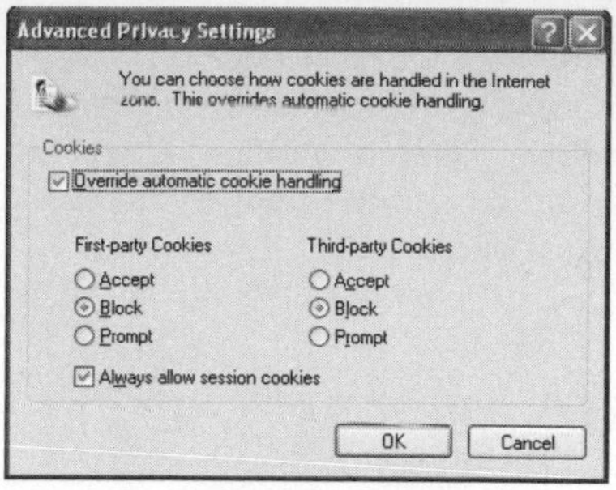

Figure 5-5

10. Click the OK button.
11. Now you should be back at the Privacy screen. Click the Sites button.
12. A window opens. In the Address of Web Site box, type the address of trustworthy websites that need cookies to function properly (Web e-mail services such as Hotmail, financial institutions such as your bank or credit-card company, e-merchants such as Amazon.com and eBay, and so on), and then click the Allow button (see Figure 5-6).

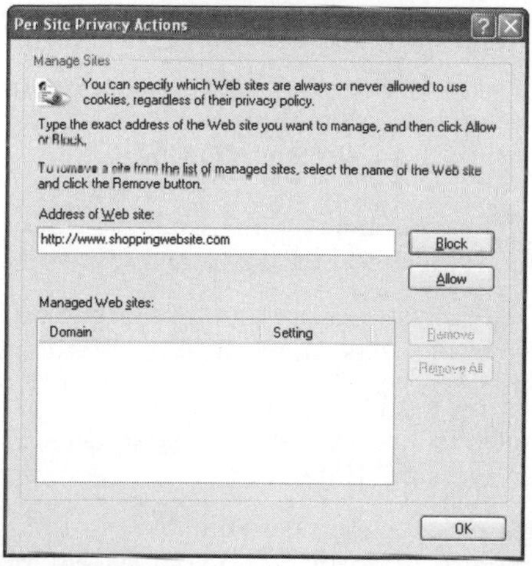

Figure 5-6

13. Type the address of any websites you do not want to receive cookies from (online advertisers like doubleclick.net, gambling sites, and so on), and then click the Block button.
14. If you change your mind about a website and want to remove it from this list, simply highlight its name, click the Remove button, and then click OK.
15. When you are finished adding or removing websites to the list, click the OK button.

Delete Tracking Cookies

To protect your privacy, you should delete the tracking cookies lurking on your computer. Because it can be difficult to identify which cookies are tracking and which are trustworthy, the easiest thing to do is simply to wipe the plate clean by erasing all of your cookies at once. Follow these steps:

1. Open Internet Explorer.
2. Click the Tools drop-down menu.
3. Select Internet Options.
4. A window opens. Under the General tab, look for Temporary Internet Files. Underneath this, click the Delete Cookies button.
5. A message pops up and asks, "Delete all cookies in the Temporary Internet Files folder?"
6. Click the OK button.
7. If other users have a Windows account on your computer, have each of them log on to their account and repeat these steps.

Delete Index Files

Even if you cover your Internet tracks by deleting tracking cookies, some information related to them can be left behind in special indexes that have the file extension .dat. To scrub these index files clean, do the following:

1. Delete all of the cookies on your computer by following the steps in the previous 5-minute fix titled "Delete Tracking Cookies."
2. Shut down your computer and restart it. After doing so, immediately press the F8 key on your keyboard several times until the Windows Advanced Options Menu screen appears.
3. Use the up or down arrow on your keyboard to select Safe Mode with Command Prompt, and then press the Enter key.
4. The next screen displays Please Select the Operating System to Start. Assuming you only have Windows XP installed on your system, press the Enter key. If you have more than one operating system installed, use the up or down arrow on your keyboard to select Windows XP, and then press the Enter key.
5. Windows loads some software, which could take a minute or two. Depending on how your version of Windows is configured, a login screen or the Welcome Screen appears. If you see the login screen, type your account name and password (if you have one), and then press the Enter key. If you see the Welcome Screen, click the icon for the account labeled Administrator or an account that has administrative privileges, and then enter your password (if you have one).
6. A command prompt appears. Type **CD** and then press the Enter key.

7. Type **del index.dat/s** and then press the Enter key.
8. Windows will delete all of your .dat files, which could take a minute or two.
9. You are returned to the command prompt. Type **shutdown –r** to force your computer to automatically shut down and restart.

Use a Firewall

To protect your computer from Internet intruders, it is crucial to use a firewall. Available in hardware and software versions, a firewall acts like a cloaking device to hide your computer from the watchful eyes of online criminals. A firewall also can filter the data that enters your computer, control Internet cookies, and warn you when sinister spyware programs try to transmit data about you over the Web. There are numerous, respected brands of hardware and software firewalls to choose from, each of which will probably suit your needs.

Note

For enhanced protection, use a hardware firewall in combination with a software firewall. If you have two or more computers networked together, using dual firewalls should stop one of the computers from spreading a worm across the network and infecting the other computers. Even if you only have one computer, using both types of firewalls together doesn't harm anything and gives you increased protection and control of the type of information your computer broadcasts over the Web.

Hardware Firewalls

These are available as stand-alone devices that sit between your computer and the Internet, and they come as a built-in feature of most routers (which are devices used to network computers together to share files and an Internet connection). Even if you have only one computer in your home or office, a router is a good, inexpensive investment, because you never know when you may purchase an additional computer and want to set up a network. Here are some popular brands of routers (in no particular order):

- Linksys BEFSR41 or BEFSX41
- NetGear RP614
- D-Link DI-604

Software Firewalls

In addition to offering many of the same features as a hardware firewall, a software firewall can alert you when a digital threat like spyware tries to connect to the Internet and transmit your data to online marketers. Also, most software firewalls let you choose which programs can or cannot access the Web. Many reputable software manufacturers have software firewalls available.

Free Firewalls

The following firewall packages are available for free:

- **Windows Firewall:** A reliable, free firewall known as Windows Firewall is included with Windows XP Service Pack 2. If your computer does not have any other software firewall installed, then Windows Firewall automatically and silently runs in the background to protect you. Although the Windows Firewall will sufficiently protect you from inbound threats that attempt to penetrate your computer, it will not alert you about any outbound threats that try to use your Internet connection. For that reason, it is not recommended.
- **ZoneAlarm Free Version:** This is one of the best software firewalls—and it won't cost you a cent. Not only does it protect against inbound and outbound threats, but it also gives you total command over the programs that are allowed to access the Internet. To download it, visit `http://www.zonelabs.com` or search for it at `http://www.download.com`.

Retail Firewalls

The following packages are available online for a nominal cost:

- ZoneAlarm Pro (`http://www.zonelabs.com`)
- Norton Internet Security (`http://www.symantec.com`)
- McAfee Personal Firewall (`http://www.mcafee.com`)
- Tiny Personal Firewall (`http://www.tinysoftware.com`)
- Desktop Firewall (`http://www.webroot.com`)
- ETrust EZ Firewall (`http://www.ca.com`)

Safely Delete Your Data

A computer file is like a road-sign that tells Windows where to locate data on your hard drive. When you delete a file and empty it from the recycle bin, you are only destroying the road-sign—not the actual data. Basically, the data just sits in limbo on your hard drive until it is overwritten by new data, which puts it at risk of being recovered by an identity thief who has the right software and computer smarts.

The only safe way to get rid of your files is to wipe them from existence—literally. Special software exists that can wipe data (also known as *shredding*), which will make the files almost impossible to recover. During the wiping process, your old files are overwritten numerous times by new, random data. Think of it like painting the same wall in your house over and over with a different color each time.

Wiping Software

You can buy professional wiping programs from retail stores or e-merchants, or you can download free ones from the Internet. The choice depends on how much (or little) money you are willing to spend and how serious you are about keeping your deleted data safe from prying eyes. Some programs give a better, more secure wipe, whereas others barely make the grade. Here are some options (in no particular order):

- File Shredder (`http://www.stompsoft.com`)
- BCWipe (`http://www.jetico.com`)
- Steganos Security Suite (`http://www.steganos.com`)

Encrypt Your Data

If a criminal steals or hacks into your computer, would he or she be able to view your private data? If you haven't encrypted your files, the answer is "Yes." If you have ever seen a spy movie, you know that encryption is the process of transforming your data into a secret code that can be viewed only by people with the correct password. With the crime of identity theft growing worse each year, encryption has become a vital part of protecting yourself from high-tech hoodlums.

Encryption Software

A variety of software manufacturers have encryption programs that you can download from the Internet. Some may take a bite out of your wallet, but others will only set you back a few bucks. Your best bet is to select one that provides reliable technical support, which will be crucial if you ever encrypt your data and then can't unlock it. Here are some encryption software you can purchase:

- BestCrypt (`http://www.jetico.com`)
- CryptoForge (`http://www.cryptoforge.com`)
- WinZip (`http://www.winzip.com`)
- Steganos Safe 8 (`http://www.steganos.com`)
- DriveCrypt (`http://www.securstar.com`)
- Turbocrypt (`http://www.pmc-ciphers.com`)
- Cryptainer (`http://www.cypherix.com`)
- Secure IT (`http://www.cypherix.com`)
- PGP Corporation (`http://www.pgp.com`)

Windows Encryption (XP Professional Edition Only)

Using XP Pro's built-in encryption software is just as easy as working with normal, everyday files.

Note

This encryption requires the NTFS file system.

Follow these steps to encrypt a file:

1. Right-click the file you want to encrypt.
2. Select Properties.
3. A window opens. Under the General tab, click the Advanced button.
4. A window opens. At the bottom of it, put a checkmark in the Encrypt Contents to Secure Data box (see Figure 5-7). If this option is grayed out, then Windows encryption is not available and you need to install a separate encryption program.

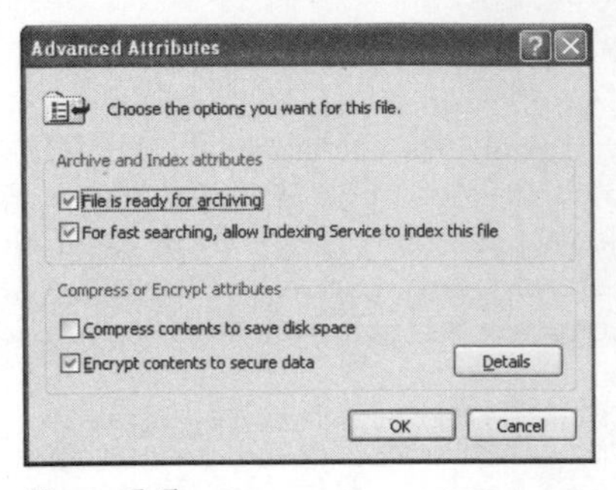

Figure 5-7

5. Click the OK button.
6. Click the Apply button.
7. A message asks you if you want to encrypt just the file or encrypt it *and* the folder it is stored in. If the file is one that you plan to make changes to, then choose to encrypt it *and* its folder. This ensures that the file remains encrypted.
8. Click the OK button.

   The name of the file has green letters instead of the usual black letters. This indicates your file is properly encrypted.

Follow these steps to encrypt a folder:

1. Right-click the folder you want to encrypt.
2. Select Properties.
3. A window opens. Under the General tab, click the Advanced button.
4. A window opens. At the bottom of it, put a checkmark in the Encrypt Contents to Secure Data box (see Figure 5-8). If this option is grayed out, then Windows encryption is not available and you need to install a separate encryption program.

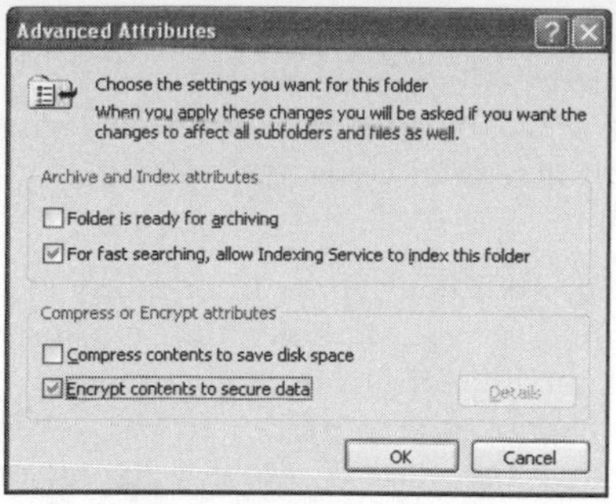

Figure 5-8

5. Click the OK button.
6. Click the Apply button.
7. A message asks you if you want to encrypt just the folder or encrypt it *and* all of the other folders inside of it (as well as the files in those other folders). If you are encrypting an important folder like My Documents, you should choose to encrypt the folder *and* its subfolders so that all of your sensitive documents are protected.
8. Click the OK button.

   The name of the folder has green letters instead of the usual black letters. This indicates your folder is properly encrypted.

Note

Any files you add to an encrypted folder automatically become encrypted.

Back Up Your Data

To preserve your computer files and prevent them from being lost forever, you should copy them to recordable or rewritable CDs/DVDs or a separate hard drive. Here are the most common reasons for data loss:

- **Dead hard drive:** The hard drives that store your files are just like any other electronic gadget — they are prone to sudden failure.
- **Killer virus:** Some digital threats lurking on the Internet have the capability of destroying certain types of files on your computer.
- **Power surge:** An electrical storm or a fluctuation in your power lines can cause a sudden burst of electricity to race into your computer and fry your hard drive and other computer parts.
- **Theft:** Computers, especially laptops, are a big target for thieves. Having your computer stolen is a double whammy because not only do you lose your data, but the thief has complete access to it and can use it to commit identity theft.

- **Fire and natural disasters:** All of your computer files can be wiped out in an instant when your home or office is destroyed by a fire, hurricane, tornado, flood, or other weather phenomenon. This makes it critical to back up your data on a regular basis and store it in a safe off-site location like a bank vault.
- **Children:** Whether your children are a few years old or a few decades old, the chances are high that at some point they will use your computer and change your settings or accidentally delete a particular document or file that has great importance to you. Prevent this by backing up your data, protecting your Windows account with a password, and setting up separate accounts for each of your family members.

Create a Disc Image

By using special software, you can create an image of your hard drive, which is a fancy way of saying that you are backing up the entire contents of your hard drive — including Windows and all software. If your hard drive ever crashes and you lose data, all you have to do is load the disc image onto your computer, and you will be up and running as if nothing ever happened. This software can be used with almost any backup device (external and internal hard drives, CD/DVD burners, and so on). Here are some popular disc-imaging programs (in no particular order):

- Norton Ghost (`http://www.symantec.com`)
- Acronis True Image (`http://www.acronis.com`)
- NTI Backup NOW (`http://www.ntius.com`)
- Turbo Backup (`http://www.filestream.com`)

Manually Back Up Your Important Files

Instead of copying your entire hard drive, the manual backup method only copies the data you consider to be irreplaceable, such as financial documents, digital photos, music files, and so on. Here are some popular programs that are used for manual backups (in no particular order):

- Nero Burning ROM or Nero Express (`http://www.nero.com`)
- NTI CD-Maker (`http://www.ntius.com`)
- Roxio Easy Media Creator (`http://www.roxio.com`)

Use Passwords

A key component in preventing intruders from accessing your Windows account is to protect it with a password. If you have not configured Windows to require a password, then follow the procedure that's applicable to your system.

For Windows XP Home Edition:

1. Click the Start button in the lower-left corner of Windows.
2. Click the Control Panel. (If you don't see this option, your Start menu is in classic mode. In that case, click Settings, and then select the Control Panel.)
3. Double-click User Accounts.
4. A window opens. Click Change an Account.
5. Select the account you want to change.
6. Click Create a Password.
7. Type a password. Do not choose a word that can easily be guessed. For more information on creating passwords that are difficult to crack, see the following 5-minute fix, "Create Strong Passwords."
8. Repeat this procedure for each Windows account. Give each user a separate, unique password.

For Windows XP Professional Edition:

1. Right-click the My Computer icon on your desktop. If this icon is not available, click the Start button in the lower-left corner of Windows and right-click My Computer. If you can't find the My Computer icon anywhere, do the following:
   a. Right-click in the empty space on your desktop.
   b. Select Properties.
   c. A window opens. Click the Desktop tab.
   d. Near the bottom of the window, click the Customize Desktop button.
   e. Another window opens. On the General tab, beneath Desktop Icons, place a checkmark in the My Computer box.
   f. Click the OK button.
   g. You are returned to the previous screen. Click the Apply button.
   h. Click the OK button.
   i. The My Computer icon appears on your desktop. Right-click it.
2. Select Manage.
3. A window opens. In the left window pane, double-click the Local Users and Groups icon.
4. Double-click the Users icon.
5. In the right window pane, right-click the account you want to change.
6. Select Set Password (see Figure 5-9).

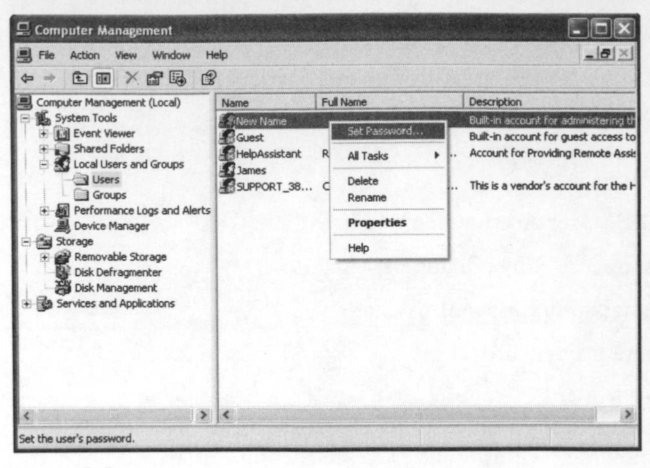

Figure 5-9

7. A window opens. Type a new, strong password for the account.

Create Strong Passwords

To keep Internet intruders from breaking into your computer, you must create strong passwords that are nearly impossible to crack. Here are some guidelines:

- If you have a simple one-word password like computer, a high-tech thief could crack it in mere minutes.
- If you make the password more robust by adding numbers — like computer33 — it might take the thief an extra 10 minutes to crack it.
- If your password is even more complex — like comPut3r55@$ — the thief would have to work around the clock for days on end before he could come close to cracking it.
- Your password should have a *minimum* of six digits, with at least *three* of the following: lowercase letters, uppercase letters, numbers, and special characters.
- The easiest way to create a strong password is to develop a pass-phrase, which is a sentence you can easily remember. Use the first letter of each word in the pass-phrase to create a password. For example, the pass-phrase "Honk if you like computer geeks" becomes the password hiylcg. To make it even stronger, use a combination of upper and lowercase letters, numbers, and special characters that look like actual letters. For example, hiylcg can be changed into h1yLc&.
- For even stronger protection, change your passwords every six months.

Avoid Certain Passwords

Because many people have a difficult time remembering their passwords, they often use names or words that are near and dear to them—like a pet's name. Although such passwords are easy to remember, they also are easy for a criminal to crack. Never use passwords containing the following:

- Nicknames for you or your family members
- A pet's name
- Your mother's maiden name
- The street number or street name of your current or former residences
- Your relatives' names
- Sequential numbers (like 1234 or 6789)
- Common words (like the word *password* or *the*)
- Words directly related to your occupation (for example, if you are a doctor, don't use *doctor*)

Use Separate Passwords

If you use online banking or shop at e-merchants' websites, then you know that you are routinely asked to create user names and passwords for those sites to prevent unauthorized people from accessing your online accounts. For convenience, the average person creates one memorable password and uses it for all the websites visited. This is a serious mistake that could lead to identity theft. Think of it this way: using a single password is like having a single key that unlocks all of the doors to your house, your cars, your fire safe, your security-deposit box at the bank, and more. If a criminal found that one key, he or she could steal all of your belongings. To ensure maximum privacy and protection when surfing the Internet, use a separate, unique password for each website.

Keep Track of Your Passwords

Here are some tips:

- Hand-write your user names and passwords on a sheet of paper and store it in your personal fire safe at your home or office. Do not type this list on your computer, because you must avoid leaving any traces of passwords on your hard drive (just in case your computer is stolen or hacked into).
- Use "vault" software. These programs act like a digital vault in which you can store, encrypt, and protect all of your passwords and user names. That way, you only have to remember one password to access all of them.

Hide the List of Recent Documents

Each time you open a document or file, Windows creates a shortcut to it that is placed in a list called Recent Documents. The purpose of this list is to give you a simple way to access your recently viewed documents without having to waste time searching for them. However, there is a downside: anyone who uses your computer—or hacks into it—can view this list to find out what documents you recently opened. To enhance your privacy and security, you can hide the Recent Documents list. Follow these steps:

1. Click the Start button in the lower-left corner of Windows.
2. Click the Control Panel. (If you don't see this option, your Start menu is in classic mode. In that case, click Settings, and then select the Control Panel.)
3. If the Control Panel is in category view, click the Appearance and Themes category, and then click the Taskbar and Start Menu icon. If the Control Panel is in classic view, simply double-click the Taskbar and Start Menu icon.
4. A window opens. Click the Start Menu tab.
5. Click the Customize button.
6. Another window opens. Click the Advanced tab.
7. Remove the checkmark from the List My Most Recently Opened Documents box.
8. Click the Clear List button.
9. Click the OK button.
10. You are returned to the previous window. Click the Apply button.
11. Click the OK button.

Disable the List of Recent Documents

Even if you followed the steps to hide the Recent Documents list, Windows XP continues to monitor the files you open or use and stores this information in the background just in case you need it. If you want to prevent Windows from keeping track of your recent documents, you must edit the Windows Registry, as follows:

1. Click the Start button in the lower-left corner of Windows.
2. Click Run.
3. A window opens. Type **regedit** in the blank, and then click the OK button or press the Enter key.
4. The Windows Registry Editor opens. In the left window pane, double-click the HKEY_CURRENT_USER registry key. If you can't find it, do the following:

a. In the left window pane of the Registry Editor, scroll to the top.

b. If any of the HKEY registry keys are open — as indicated by a minus sign (-) on their left side — then close them by clicking that minus sign. When a registry key is properly closed, it has a plus sign (+) next to it.

c. Repeat this process for the remaining HKEY registry keys until the only things visible in the left window pane are the five HKEY keys (see Figure 5-10).

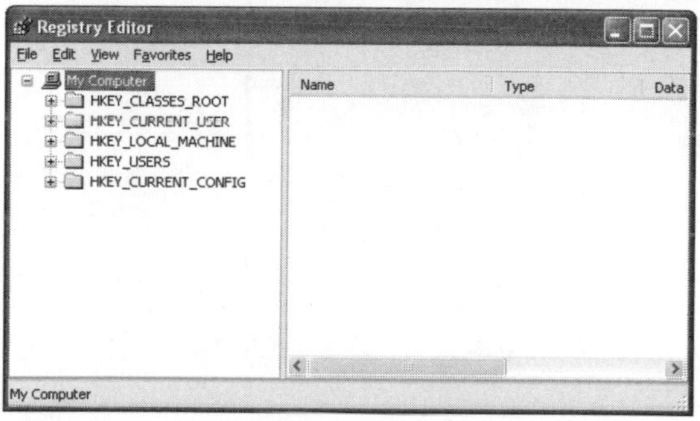

Figure 5-10

d. Double-click the HKEY_CURRENT_USER registry key.

5. A new column of registry keys appears. Double-click Software.

6. Another list of registry keys appears. Scroll down and double-click Microsoft.

7. A long column of registry keys appears. Scroll down and double-click Windows.

8. Double-click the CurrentVersion registry key.

9. A new column of registry keys appears. Scroll down and double-click Policies.

10. Click the Explorer registry key (see Figure 5-11).

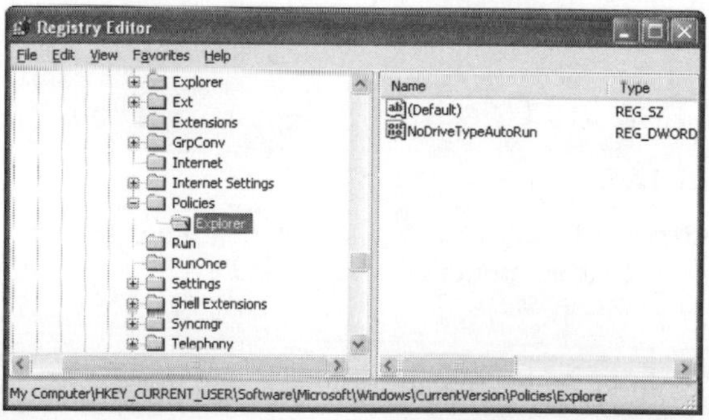

Figure 5-11

11. Click the Edit drop-down menu located in the upper-left corner of the Windows Registry Editor.
12. Select New.
13. Select DWORD Value.
14. In the right window pane, a new registry value appears. Rename it **NoRecentDocsHistory** (see Figure 5-12).

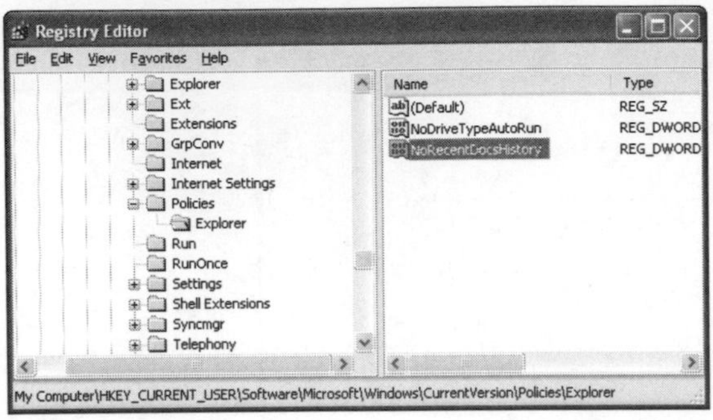

Figure 5-12

15. Double-click new NoRecentDocsHistory value to open it.
16. Type the number **1** under the Value Data heading.
17. Click the OK button.
18. Exit the Registry Editor by clicking the X button in the upper-right corner.
19. If you want to undo this fix and restore the list of recent documents, do the following:
    a. Open the Windows Registry Editor and return to the NoRecentDocsHistory registry value you created.
    b. Double-click this registry value to open it.
    c. Under the Value Data heading labeled, delete the number 1. Type the number **0** in its place.

Erase the List of Recent Documents When Exiting Windows

If you prefer to keep the Recent Documents list, you can still enhance your privacy by modifying the list so that its contents are emptied every time you exit Windows. Here's how:

1. Click the Start button in the lower-left corner of Windows.
2. Click Run.

3. A window opens. Type **regedit** in the blank, and then click the OK button or press the Enter key.

4. The Windows Registry Editor opens. In the left window pane, double-click the HKEY_CURRENT_USER registry key. If you can't find it, do the following:

   a. In the left window pane of the Registry Editor, scroll to the top.

   b. If any of the HKEY registry keys are open — as indicated by a minus sign (-) on their left side — then close them by clicking that minus sign. When a registry key is properly closed, it has a plus sign (+) next to it.

   c. Repeat this process for the remaining HKEY registry keys until the only things visible in the left window pane are the five HKEY keys (see Figure 5-13).

   d. Double-click the HKEY_CURRENT_USER registry key.

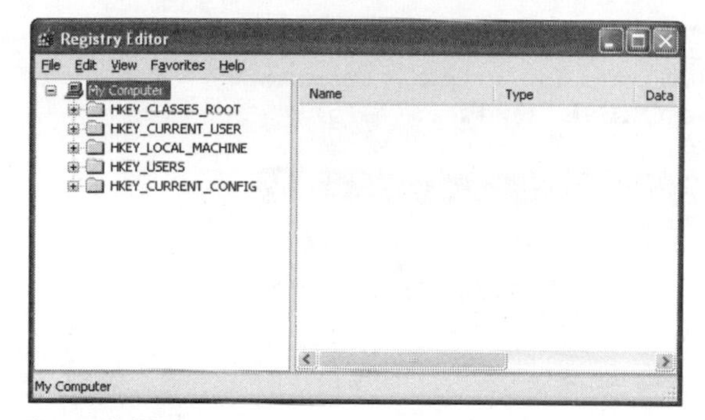

Figure 5-13

5. A new column of registry keys appears. Double-click Software.

6. Another list of registry keys appears. Scroll down and double-click Microsoft.

7. A long column of registry keys appears. Scroll down and double-click Windows.

8. Double-click the CurrentVersion registry key.

9. A new column of registry keys appears. Scroll down and double-click Policies.

10. Click the Explorer registry key (see Figure 5-14).

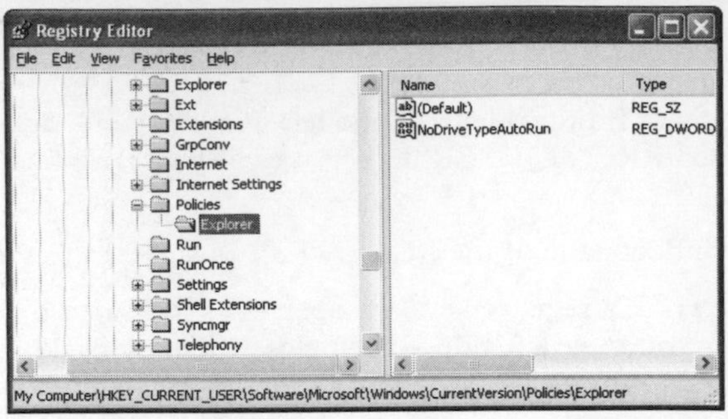

Figure 5-14

11. Click the Edit drop-down menu located in the upper-left corner of the Windows Registry Editor.
12. Select New.
13. Select DWORD Value.
14. In the right window pane, a new registry value appears. Rename it **ClearRecentDocsOnExit** (see Figure 5-15).

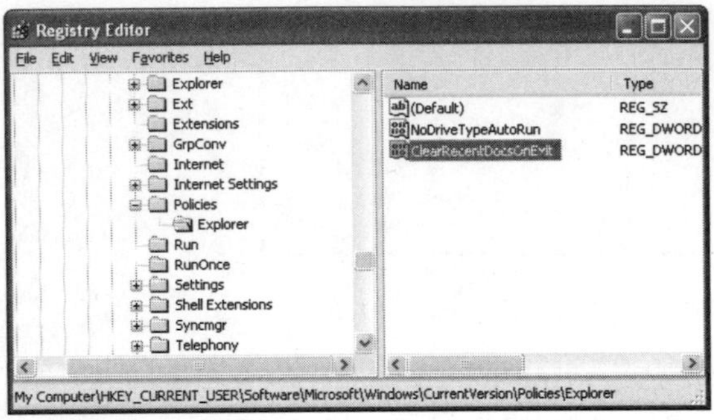

Figure 5-15

15. Double-click the new ClearRecentDocsOnExit value to open it.
16. Type the number **1** under the Value Data heading.
17. Click the OK button.
18. Exit the Registry Editor by clicking the X button in the upper-right corner.
19. If you want to undo this fix and restore the list of recent documents to its original settings, do the following:
    a. Open the Windows Registry Editor and return to the ClearRecentDocsOnExit registry value you created.
    b. Double-click this registry value to open it.
    c. Under the Value Data heading, delete the number 1. Type the number **0** in its place.

6

CLEAN A CLUTTERED DESKTOP

Is your Windows desktop so jam-packed with shortcuts, folders, and files that you can barely see the desktop wallpaper peeking out from behind them? Perhaps it is time for a digital Spring cleaning. To cut the clutter and restore order to your desktop, follow the 5-minute fixes in this chapter.

Use the Quick Launch Toolbar

Windows XP has a feature known as Quick Launch that allows you to quickly access your programs without having to clutter your desktop with countless shortcuts. Here's how to use it:

1. Right-click the empty space on the taskbar (which is the strip between your Start button and the Windows clock).
2. Select Toolbars.
3. Select Quick Launch.
4. The Quick Launch toolbar appears next to the Start button. This toolbar allows you to access shortcuts to commonly used programs. One of its best features is the handy shortcut known as Show Desktop (see Figure 6-1). When you click this button, the desktop immediately appears. This can be quite useful when you have several programs or files open and you want to access something on your desktop. Instead of minimizing each individual program or file to reveal the desktop, you can simply click this shortcut.

Do It Yourself

Figure 6-1

5. To decrease the clutter on your desktop, you can move its icons and shortcuts to the Quick Launch toolbar. Simply *drag* the icon from your desktop to the Quick Launch and *drop* it next to one of the other Quick Launch icons (see Figure 6-2).

Figure 6-2

To make this process even easier, click the small vertical column of dots located on the right side of the Quick Launch and drag it to the right (see Figure 6-3). This increases the size of your Quick Launch toolbar and gives you more room for dragging and dropping.

Figure 6-3

6. After transferring the desktop shortcuts to the Quick Launch, you can organize them in whatever order you desire. To do so, click one of the shortcuts and hold down your mouse button. Next, drag the shortcut left or right on the Quick Launch toolbar to a position that suits you.
7. To remove a shortcut from the Quick Launch, right-click the shortcut and select Delete. When you see a message asking whether or not you want to send the shortcut to the Recycle Bin, click the Yes button.
8. Moving a shortcut to the Quick Launch Toolbar does not remove its original version from your desktop. To clean up the clutter on your desktop, right-click the original shortcut and select Delete. When you see a message asking whether or not you want to send the shortcut to the Recycle Bin, click the Yes button.
9. When you are finished modifying the Quick Launch, consider locking it, which gives your desktop a cleaner look. Simply right-click the empty space on the taskbar and select Lock the Taskbar. This is merely a suggestion to make Windows more neat and tidy. Nothing bad will happen if you choose not to lock the Quick Launch toolbar.

Restore the Show Desktop Shortcut

If you follow the steps to turn on the Quick Launch toolbar, you will discover that its Show Desktop shortcut is the fastest way to jump from a program or folder to your desktop. This is particularly handy when you have multiple windows or programs open and you need to view a file stored on your desktop.

Be careful not to accidentally delete the Show Desktop shortcut, because you cannot restore it by normal means. Instead, you will need to create a special file by using the Windows Notepad, like this:

1. Click the Start button in the lower-left corner of Windows.
2. Click the Control Panel. (If you don't see this option, your Start menu is in classic mode. In that case, click Settings, and then select the Control Panel.)
3. If the Control Panel is in category view, click the Appearance and Themes category, and then click the Folder Options icon. If the Control Panel is in classic view, simply double-click the Folder Options icon.
4. A window opens. Click the View tab.
5. Under the Advanced Settings heading, scroll down and click the Show Hidden Files and Folders button.
6. Click the Apply button.
7. Click the OK button.
8. Now you must locate Notepad. Click the Start button in the lower-left corner of Windows.
9. Click All Programs.
10. Select Accessories.
11. Click Notepad.
12. A blank document opens in Notepad. Type **[shell]** and then press the Enter key.
13. Type **Command=2** and then press the Enter key.
14. Type **IconFile=explorer.exe.3** and then press Enter.
15. Type **[Taskbar]** and then press Enter.
16. Type **Command=ToggleDesktop** and then double check all five lines of text to make sure they look exactly like Figure 6-4.

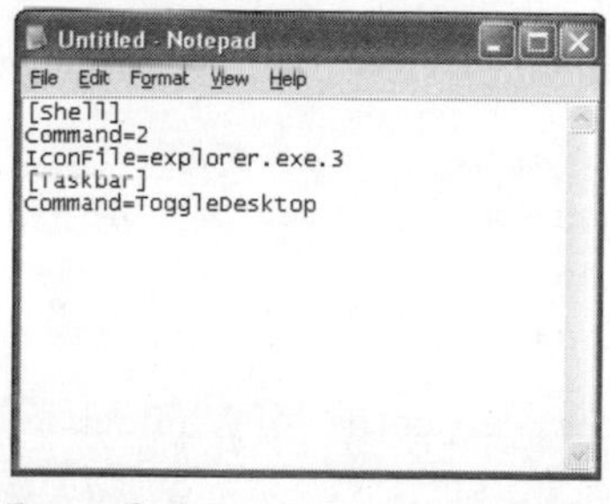

Figure 6-4

17. Click the File drop-down menu located in the upper-left corner of Notepad.

18. Select Save.

19. A window opens, asking you to give the file a name. Type **Show Desktop.scf** (see Figure 6-5).

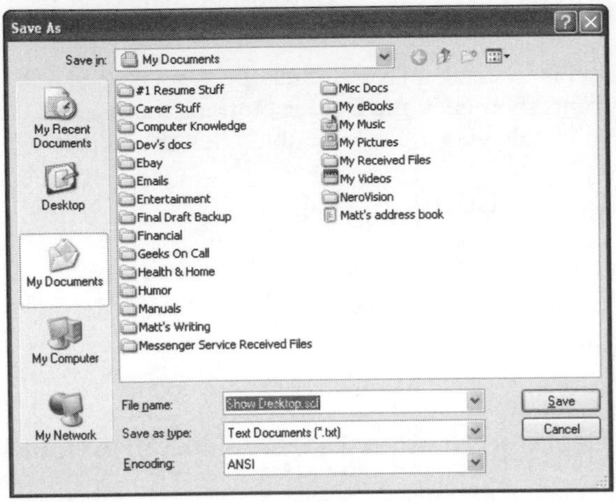

Figure 6-5

20. You must select a location where the file will be saved. In the browsing window, double-click the My Computer icon.

21. Double-click the icon for your C: drive (unless you installed Windows in a different location, in which case, double-click that drive letter).

22. Double-click the Documents and Settings folder.

23. Double-click the folder containing the name of your Windows account. For example, if your account is named Bob, then double-click the Bob folder.

24. Double-click the Application Data folder.

25. Double click the Microsoft folder.

26. Double-click the Internet Explorer folder.

27. Double-click the Quick Launch folder.

28. Now that you have given this file a name and have selected the location to save it in, click the Save button.

29. Re-hide the special system files and folders, as follows:

    a. Click the Start button in the lower-left corner of Windows.

    b. Click the Control Panel. (If you don't see this option, your Start menu is in classic mode. In that case, click Settings, and then select the Control Panel.)

c. If the Control Panel is in category view, click the Appearance and Themes category, and then click the Folder Options icon. If the Control Panel is in classic view, simply double-click the Folder Options icon.

d. A window opens. Click the View tab.

e. Under the Advanced Settings heading, scroll down and click the Do Not Show Hidden Files and Folders button.

f. Click the Apply button.

g. Click the OK button.

Add or Remove the My Computer and My Documents Shortcuts

By default, a new installation of Windows XP does not litter the desktop with countless shortcuts (which older versions of Windows were notorious for doing). This means that popular icons and destinations like My Computer and My Documents are not automatically available on the desktop. If you prefer to have them there, they can be easily restored. On the other hand, if you are more interested in clearing the clutter from your desktop, you can delete these shortcuts and instead access them through the Start menu.

To add the My Computer or the My Documents shortcuts, follow these steps:

1. Right-click in the empty space on your desktop.
2. Select Properties.
3. A window opens. Click the Desktop tab.
4. Near the bottom of the window, click the Customize Desktop button.
5. Another window opens. On the General tab, beneath Desktop Icons, place checkmarks in the My Computer box and the My Documents box.
6. Click the OK button.
7. You are returned to the previous screen. Click the Apply button.
8. Click the OK button.
9. The My Computer icon appears on your desktop.

To remove the My Computer and/or the My Documents shortcuts, follow these steps:

1. Right-click the shortcut you want to remove and select Delete, or drag and drop it into the Recycle Bin.
2. A message pops up and asks, "Are you sure you want to delete the icon from your desktop?" Click the Yes button.

3. To access My Computer or My Documents, simply click the Start button in the lower-left corner of Windows.

Rearrange Your Desktop Shortcuts

Most computers running Windows XP automatically use a feature known as Align to Grid that attempts to bring order to your desktop by stacking your shortcuts in clean, evenly-spaced rows and columns. Unfortunately, this feature prevents you from customizing the look of your desktop. Many people enjoy the ability to freely move their shortcuts anywhere because it makes their desktops feel less cluttered and allows more of their desktop wallpaper to be seen. To arrange your shortcuts how ever you want, turn off the Align to Grid option as follows:

1. Right-click the empty space on your desktop.
2. Select Arrange Icons By.
3. Select Align to Grid.
4. Now you can arrange your shortcuts anyway you want by clicking them and dragging them to any spot on your desktop. To enhance the beauty of your desktop wallpaper and show as much of it as possible, consider placing your icons along the edges of the desktop.

Restore Missing Desktop Icons

If every icon on your desktop has suddenly vanished, don't panic — you may have accidentally told Windows to hide them. Fortunately, this is easily reversed. Here's how:

1. Right-click the empty space on your desktop.
2. Select Arrange Icons By.
3. Select Show Desktop Icons.

7

5-Minute Fixes™

ORGANIZE YOUR DIGITAL LIFE

Do you have difficulty finding files on your computer? Does your hard drive resemble a "junk drawer" — a place to store all kinds of knickknacks and odds and ends? To make Windows XP more efficient and productive and to organize your digital life, follow the 5-minute fixes in this chapter.

Alphabetize Your Bookmarks

One of the easiest ways to rearrange your jumbled collection of Internet Explorer bookmarks is to alphabetize them as follows:

1. Open Internet Explorer.
2. Click the Favorites drop-down menu.
3. Right-click any bookmark or folder.
4. Select Sort by Name.

Change the Lineup of Your Bookmarks

To give yourself quick access to your frequently used bookmarks, you can rearrange them so that your favorite ones are placed at the top of the lineup. Here's how:

1. Open Internet Explorer.
2. Click the Favorites drop-down menu.
3. Click the name of a bookmark or folder.
4. Hold down the mouse button and *drag* the bookmark or folder up or down the lineup until it's in a position that suits you. Then release the mouse button to *drop* the bookmark or folder into the new location. (This action is referred to as *drag-and-drop* and is used throughout this chapter.)

Do It Yourself

Organize Your Bookmarks

If you use the Internet on a regular basis, you probably have accumulated a large collection of miscellaneous bookmarks. To avoid the hassle of scouring your entire collection to find one specific bookmark—which could make finding a needle in a haystack seem easy—you can separate and organize them with a few simple techniques:

1. Double-click the My Computer icon on your desktop. If this icon is not available, then click the Start button in the lower-left corner of Windows and click My Computer. If you can't find the My Computer icon anywhere, do the following:
    a. Right-click in the empty space on your desktop.
    b. Select Properties.
    c. A window opens. Click the Desktop tab.
    d. Near the bottom of the window, click the Customize Desktop button.
    e. Another window opens. On the General tab, beneath Desktop Icons, place a checkmark in the My Computer box.
    f. Click the OK button.
    g. You are returned to the previous screen. Click the Apply button.
    h. Click the OK button.
    i. The My Computer icon appears on your desktop. Double-click it.
2. A window opens. Double-click the icon for your C: drive (unless you installed Windows in a different location, in which case you would double-click that drive letter).
3. Double-click the Documents and Settings folder.
4. Double-click the folder containing the name of your Windows account. For example, if your account is named Bob, then double-click the Bob folder.
5. Double-click the Favorites folder, which contains your bookmarks.
6. Some bookmarks have long names that are difficult to read. To give a bookmark a shorter name, right-click it, select Rename, and then type a new name.
7. To make it easier to find a particular bookmark while surfing the Internet, you can organize your bookmarks into separate folders with easily identifiable names as follows:
    a. Click the File drop-down menu located in the upper-left corner of the Favorites folder.
    b. Select New.
    c. Select Folder.

   d. A New Folder appears. Type a name for it that indicates what kind of bookmarks it will contain. For example, you could call the folder Shopping and use it to store all of the bookmarks to your favorite Internet stores.

   e. Repeat this process until you have created enough unique folders to store your different types of bookmarks.

   f. If you change your mind and want to give a folder a different name, right-click it, select Rename, and then type a new name.

8. Now you can begin to move your bookmarks into the folders you created:

   a. To move a single bookmark, click it, and then drag-and-drop it onto a folder.

   b. To move several bookmarks at once, hold down the Ctrl key while clicking the names of each bookmark. Once all relevant bookmarks are highlighted, drag-and-drop them onto a folder.

Enhance Your Folders

Instead of wasting time clicking through one drop-down menu after another until you find the Windows feature you want, you can make your folders more user friendly by adding shortcuts to commonly used commands. Follow these steps:

Note

Any changes you make will be applied to all of your folders.

1. Double-click any folder to open it.
2. Click the View drop-down menu.
3. Select Toolbars.
4. Select Customize.
5. The Customize Toolbar window opens. In the left window pane, under the Available Toolbar Buttons heading, scroll down and click Cut (see Figure 7-1).

Figure 7-1

6. In the middle of the window, click the Add button.

7. The Cut icon will appear in the Current Toolbar Buttons window pane on the right (see Figure 7-2). To change its position in your folders' toolbars, click the Move Up or Move Down button. Each time you click one of these buttons, the icon moves one space up the list or one space down the list.

   The higher you place the icon, the farther to the left it will appear in your folders' toolbars. The lower you place the icon, the farther to the right it will appear in your folders' toolbars.

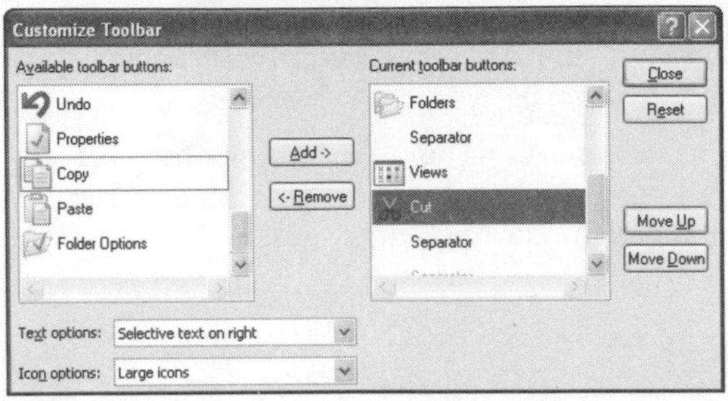

Figure 7-2

8. Repeat this procedure for the Copy, Paste, and Delete icons, and for any other options you want to add to your folders' toolbars.

9. If you change your mind and want to delete an icon from the list, select it, and then click the Remove button.

10. To separate the icons from one another or to arrange them in groups, you can add thin vertical lines known as *separators*. Here's how:

    a. Under the Available Toolbar Buttons heading, click the Separator icon (see Figure 7-3).

    b. Add it to the right window pane in the same way you added the other icons.

    c. Change the separator's position by clicking the Move Up or Move Down button.

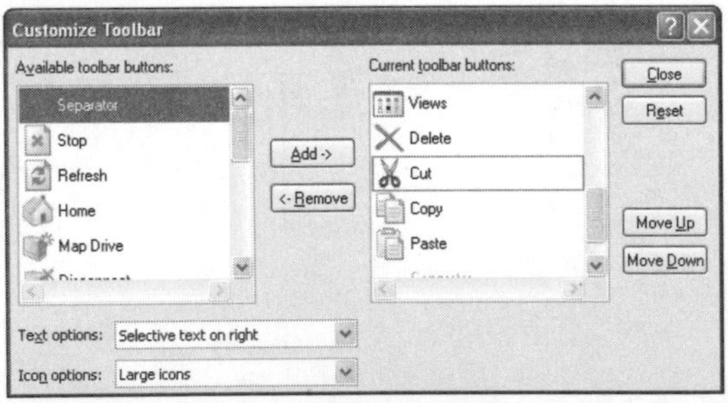

Figure 7-3

   d. To add more separators, repeat this process until the toolbar is organized to your liking.

11. To help you identify the icons, you can place names next to them. Click the drop-down menu labeled Text Options.
   a. If you want all of the icons to have names, select Show Text Labels.
   b. If you want just the important icons to have names, select Selective Text on Right.
   c. If you do not want any names to be displayed, select No Text Labels.
12. When you are finished customizing the toolbar, click the Close button.

Turn on the Status Bar

The Status Bar is a feature of Windows that provides extra details about the files or folders you are viewing (see Figure 7-4). It also comes in handy when you're using Internet Explorer, because it enables you to roll your mouse cursor over a hyperlink and see the actual Web address for that link.

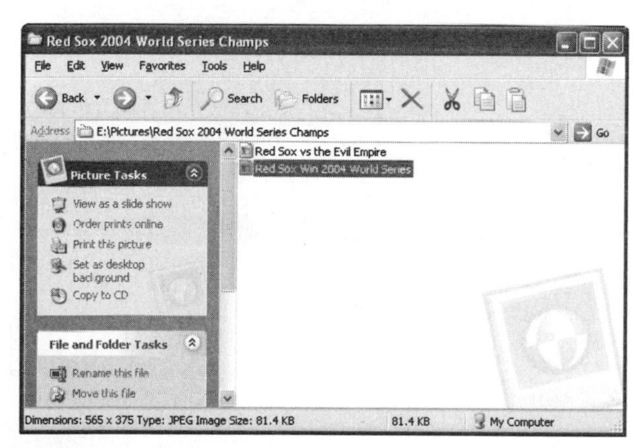

Figure 7-4

Note

Any changes you make to the Status Bar will be applied to all of your folders.

Follow these steps to display the Status Bar on Windows XP:

1. Double-click any folder to open it.
2. Click the View drop-down menu.
3. Click Status Bar.
4. The status bar will appear at the bottom of your folder.

Follow these steps to display the Status Bar in Internet Explorer:

1. Open Internet Explorer.
2. Click the View drop-down menu.
3. Select Status Bar.

Turn on the Address Bar

A great way to zip back and forth between your hard drives, CD/DVD drives, and important folders like My Documents is to use the Address Bar. If you haven't turned on this feature, here's how:

Note

Any changes you make to the Address Bar will be applied to all of your folders.

1. Double-click any folder to open it.
2. Click the View drop-down menu.
3. Select Toolbars.
4. Select Address Bar.
5. The Address Bar appears near the top of your folder. To move quickly from your current folder to a different location on your computer—such as My Documents or your CD or DVD drive—click the drop-down menu on the Address Bar and select the name of your desired destination (see Figure 7-5).

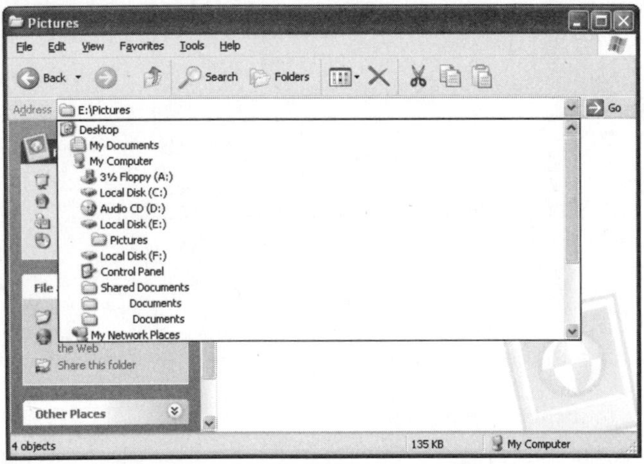

Figure 7-5

Get Organized with New Folders

You have probably noticed that Windows XP encourages you to save your files and downloads in the My Documents folder. As a result, that folder can quickly overflow with a flood of random, unorganized data. To cut through the chaos and restore order to this or any other folder, you can create new folders and subfolders. Follow these steps:

1. Double-click the My Computer icon on your desktop. If this icon is not available, then click the Start button in the lower-left corner of Windows and click My Computer. If you can't find the My Computer icon anywhere, do the following:
    a. Right-click in the empty space on your desktop.
    b. Select Properties.
    c. A window opens. Click the Desktop tab.
    d. Near the bottom of the window, click the Customize Desktop button.
    e. Another window opens. On the General tab, beneath Desktop Icons, place a checkmark in the My Computer box.
    f. Click the OK button.
    g. You are returned to the previous screen. Click the Apply button.
    h. Click the OK button.
    i. The My Computer icon appears on your desktop. Double-click it.
2. A window opens. Double-click the icon for your C: drive (unless you installed Windows in a different location, in which case you would double-click that drive letter).
3. Click the File drop-down menu.
4. Select New.
5. Select Folder.
6. A new folder appears. Type a name for it that indicates what kind of files it will contain. For example, you could call the folder Downloads and use it to temporarily store all of the files and programs you download from the Internet until you can find permanent places for them. Another possibility is a folder named Installers in which you store the various installer programs for software you purchase from Internet stores.
7. Repeat this process until you create enough unique folders to store your different types of files and programs.
8. If you change your mind and want to give a folder a different name, right-click it, select Rename, and then type a new name.

Create Desktop Shortcuts for Folders

A speedy way to access frequently-used folders is to place shortcuts to them directly on your desktop. Here's how:

1. Double-click the My Computer icon on your desktop. If this icon is not available, then click the Start button in the lower-left corner of Windows and click My Computer. If you can't find the My Computer icon anywhere, do the following:
    a. Right-click in the empty space on your desktop.
    b. Select Properties.
    c. A window opens. Click the Desktop tab.
    d. Near the bottom of the window, click the Customize Desktop button.
    e. Another window opens. On the General tab, beneath Desktop Icons, place a checkmark in the My Computer box.
    f. Click the OK button.
    g. You are returned to the previous screen. Click the Apply button.
    h. Click the OK button.
    i. The My Computer icon appears on your desktop. Double-click it.
2. A window opens. Double-click the icon for the hard drive containing your frequently-used folders (most likely this will be your C: drive).
3. Locate a folder you open constantly (such as the Downloads folder you might have created by following the "Easily Locate Your Downloads" 5-minute fix in Chapter 3).
4. Right-click the folder and select Send To.
5. Select Desktop (Create Shortcut). The new shortcut appears on your desktop.
6. You can change the name of the shortcut to make it shorter.
    a. Return to your desktop.
    b. Right-click the shortcut and select Rename.
    c. Type a new name. For example, if your shortcut is named Shortcut to Downloads, you can simply rename it Downloads.

You can keep your desktop free of clutter by transferring the new shortcut to the Quick Launch toolbar. For more information, please refer to the 5-minute fix titled "Use the Quick Launch Toolbar" in Chapter 6.

Create Desktop Shortcuts for Windows Programs

Most software gives you the option to create shortcuts to it that will be placed on your desktop. However, by default, Windows XP does not automatically do this for its frequently-used programs like Notepad, Paint, Calculator, System Restore, Disk Defragmenter, and so on. To access these programs quickly and easily, you can create shortcuts to them, as follows:

1. Click the Start button in the lower-left corner of Windows.
2. Click All Programs.
3. Select Accessories.
4. Right-click a frequently used program like Notepad or Paint, and then select Send To.
5. Select Desktop (Create Shortcut). The new shortcut appears on your desktop.
6. You can change the name of the shortcut to make it easier to understand, like this:
    a. Return to your desktop.
    b. Right-click the shortcut and select Rename.
    c. Type a new name.

You can keep your desktop free of clutter by transferring the new shortcut to the Quick Launch toolbar. For more information, please refer to the 5-minute fix titled "Use the Quick Launch Toolbar" in Chapter 6.

Unfreeze the Disk Cleanup Program

On many Windows XP computers, the Disk Cleanup program froze within seconds of launching. Normally it should only take a minute or two for it to analyze your computer and provide a list of things to delete, so if several minutes have elapsed and nothing seems to be happening, try this fix:

1. Double-click the My Computer icon on your desktop. If this icon is not available, click the Start button in the lower-left corner of Windows and click My Computer. If you can't find the My Computer icon anywhere, do the following:
    a. Right-click in the empty space on your desktop.
    b. Select Properties.
    c. A window opens. Click the Desktop tab.
    d. Click the Customize Desktop button near the bottom of the window.
    e. Another window opens. On the General tab, beneath Desktop Icons, place a checkmark in the My Computer box.

   f. Click the OK button.

   g. You are returned to the previous screen. Click the Apply button.

   h. Click the OK button.

   i. The My Computer icon appears on your desktop. Double-click it.

2. A window opens. Right-click the name of the drive you want to clean up.

3. Select Properties.

4. A new window opens. Under the General tab, click the Disk Cleanup button. This launches the Disk Cleanup program.

If the Disk Cleanup program continues to freeze, you can fix the problem once and for all by editing the Windows Registry. Here's how:

1. Click the Start button in the lower-left corner of Windows.

2. Click Run.

3. A window opens. Type **regedit** in the blank, and then click the OK button or press the Enter key.

4. The Windows Registry Editor opens. In the left window pane, double-click the HKEY_LOCAL_MACHINE registry key. If you can't find it, do the following:

   a. In the left window pane of the Registry Editor, scroll to the top.

   b. If any of the HKEY registry keys are open—as indicated by a minus sign (-) on their left side—then close them by clicking that minus sign. When a registry key is properly closed, it has a plus sign (+) next to it.

   c. Repeat this process for the remaining HKEY registry keys until the only things visible in the left window pane are the five HKEY keys (see Figure 7-6).

   d. Double-click the HKEY_LOCAL_MACHINE registry key.

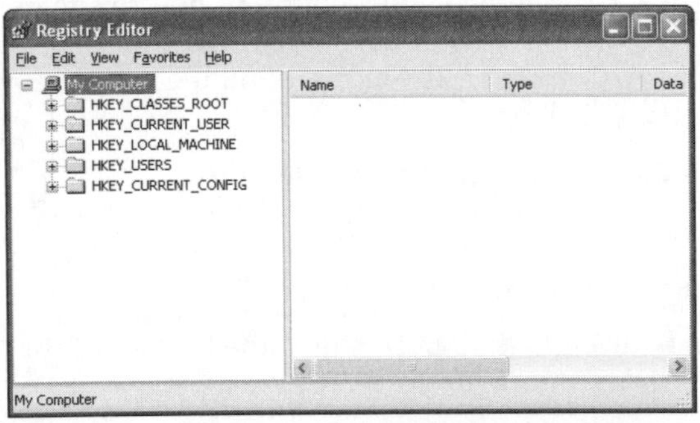

Figure 7-6

5. A new column of registry keys appears. Double-click Software.
6. Another list of registry keys appears. Scroll down and double-click Microsoft.
7. A long column of registry keys appears. Scroll down and double-click Windows.
8. Double-click the CurrentVersion registry key.
9. Double-click the Explorer registry key.
10. A new column of registry keys appears. Scroll down and double-click VolumeCaches.
11. Right-click the Compress Old Files registry key, and then select Delete (see Figure 7-7).

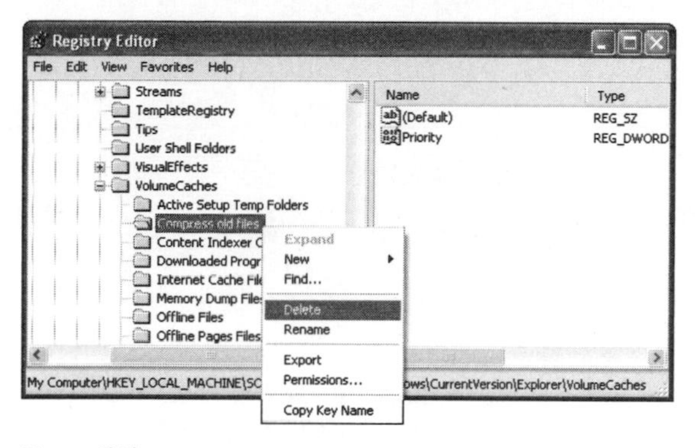

Figure 7-7

12. You are asked to confirm the deletion. Click the Yes button.
13. Exit the Registry Editor by clicking the X button in the upper-right corner.

FYI

Don't take chances with programs that clean the Windows Registry, because usually they do more harm than good. To prevent Windows from becoming damaged or corrupt, you should consider using a Registry cleaner only if your computer is experiencing severe problems like crashes or freezes.

View File Details

A handy way to receive quick information about your files — such as the size of a document or the audio quality of a digital song — is to view them in the Details mode. Follow these steps:

1. Open a folder by double-clicking it.
2. Click the View drop-down menu located at the top of the folder.
3. Select Details. This causes several columns of details to appear next to your files. To change the kind of details that are displayed, do the following:

a. Click the View drop-down menu located at the top of the folder.

b. Select Choose Details.

c. A window opens, listing all possible columns that can be displayed (see Figure 7-8). To add a new detail, place a checkmark in the box next to it. To get rid of a detail, remove the checkmark from the box next to it.

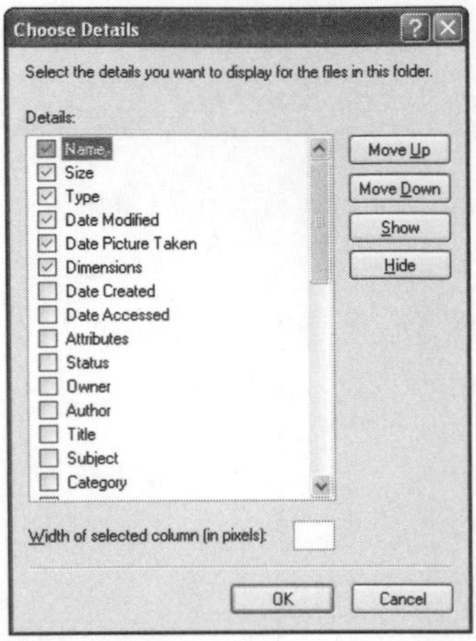

Figure 7-8

d. To change the order in which the columns of details are displayed, click the Move Up and Move Down buttons. Placing a detail lower on this list shifts it toward the right side of your folder. Placing a detail higher on this list moves it toward the left side of your folder.

e. When the detail list is in the order you want it, click the OK button.

4. Sometimes the columns of details can overlap each other and prevent you from clearly viewing their information. To automatically resize them so that all of their information can be seen without any wasted space, do the following:

   a. Click anywhere in the empty space inside the folder.

   b. Press the Ctrl key.

   c. While holding down Ctrl, and press the + key on the number pad (located on the right side of your keyboard).

Get Quick Dimensions of Digital Photos

An easy way to determine the size and format of your digital photos is to view them as Tiles, like this:

1. Open a folder by double-clicking it.
2. Click the View drop-down menu located at the top of the folder.
3. Select Tiles. Beneath the name of each photo, there is a brief description of its format (such as JPEG, Bitmap, TIF, or GIF Image) followed by the dimensions of the picture (such as 800 × 600 or 1024 × 768), as shown in Figure 7-9.

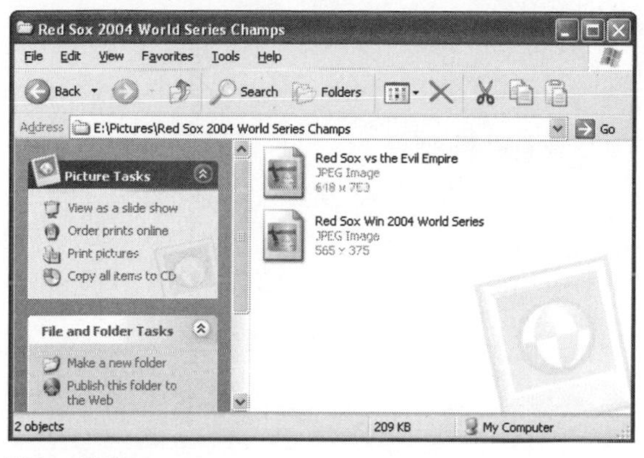

Figure 7-9

View Thumbnails of Digital Photos

Undoubtedly the best way to display digital photos in a folder is to use the thumbnail view. A thumbnail is a miniature version of your photo that allows you to see what the picture looks like without opening it. This is particularly handy when you need to find a photo in a hurry but cannot remember its file name.

1. Open a folder by double-clicking it.
2. Click the View drop-down menu located at the top of the folder.
3. Select Thumbnails.

Show Files in Groups

To arrange and manage your files more easily, use the Show Files in Groups feature, as follows:

1. Open a folder by double-clicking it.
2. Click the View drop-down menu located at the top of the folder.
3. If the files in your folder are currently displayed as Thumbnails, Tiles, Icons, or Details, then proceed to Step 4. If your files are displayed as a List, then select one of the other views, because the Show Files in Groups feature does not work with lists.

4. Select Arrange Files By.
5. Select Show in Groups. This causes similar files to be grouped underneath a heading that clearly identifies them (see Figure 7-10).

Figure 7-10

8

5-Minute Fixes

UNLOCK THE HIDDEN POWER OF XP

The slogan for the 1980s *Transformers* toys and cartoons was "More Than Meets the Eye." Similarly, Windows XP has more to offer than it might appear. Tucked away behind its familiar exterior are several powerful features that most XP users don't even know exist. To harness this power, follow the 5-minute fixes in this chapter.

Do It Yourself

Print a Directory of Files or Folders

There may come a time when you need to print a reference showing the names of the files or folders stored on your computer. Since this feature is not built into Windows XP, you will have to add it with the help of this handy fix:

1. Click the Start button in the lower-left corner of Windows.
2. Click on All Programs.
3. Select Accessories.
4. Click Notepad.
5. A blank document opens in Notepad. Type **@echo off** and then press the Enter key.
6. Type **dir %1 /-p /o:gn > "%temp%\Listing"** and then press the Enter key.
7. Type **start /w notepad /p "%temp%\Listing"** and then press the Enter key.
8. Type **del "%temp%\Listing"** and then press the Enter key.
9. Type **exit** and then double check all five lines of text to make sure they look exactly like Figure 8-1.

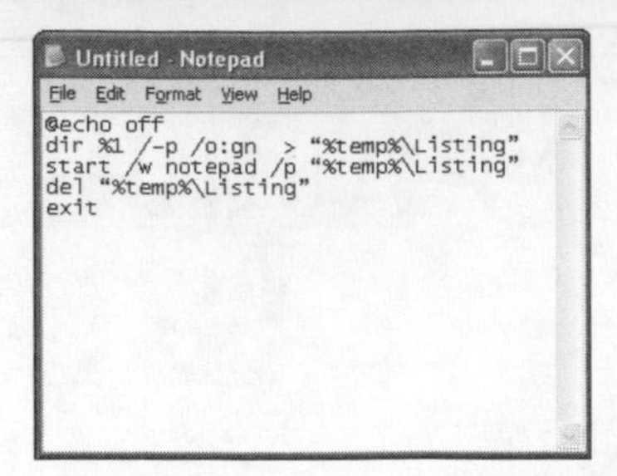

Figure 8-1

10. Click the File drop-down menu located in the upper-left corner of Notepad, and then select Exit.
11. A message alerts you that "The text in the untitled file has changed—Do you want to save the changes?" If you see this message, click the Yes button.
12. A window opens, asking you to give the file a name. Type **%windir%\Printdir.bat** and then click the Save button.
13. Click the Start button in the lower-left corner of Windows.
14. Click the Control Panel. (If you don't see this option, your Start menu is in classic mode. In that case, click Settings, and then select the Control Panel.)
15. If the Control Panel is in category view, click the Appearance and Themes category, and then click the Folder Options icon. If the Control Panel is in classic view, simply double-click the Folder Options icon.
16. A window opens. Click the File Types tab.
17. Under the Registered File Types heading, click File Types. This lists the file types alphabetically.
18. Scroll down the list until you see the File Folder file type, and then click it to select it (see Figure 8-2). Be sure not to confuse this file type with the one Folder file type located a few rows below it.
19. Click the Advanced button located near the lower-right corner of this window.
20. A new window opens. Click the New button.
21. Another window opens. Type **Print Directory Listing** in the Action blank.
22. Type **printdir.bat** in the Application blank.
23. Click the OK button.
24. You are returned to the previous window. Click the OK button.
25. Back in the Folder Options window, click the Close button.
26. To test your new print directory feature, turn on your printer, right-click a folder, and then select Print Directory Listing.

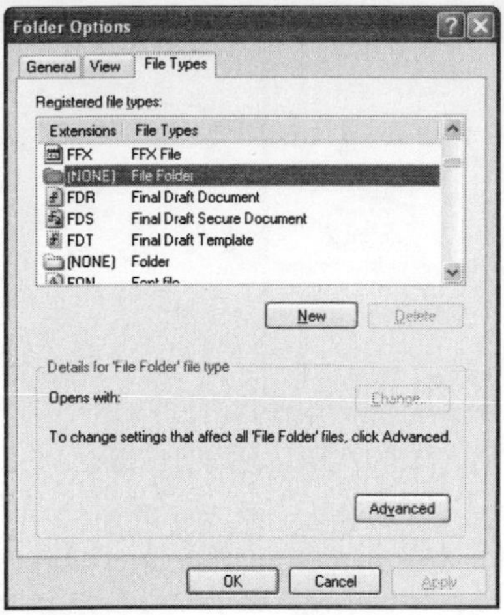

Figure 8-2

Because of these modifications, it is likely that whenever you double-click a folder, you will not be able to open it. Instead, the Windows Search Companion or another program may launch. To restore your ability to open a folder by double-clicking it, you need to edit the Windows registry. Follow these steps.

1. Click the Start button in the lower-left corner of Windows.
2. Click Run.
3. A window opens. Type **regedit** in the blank, and then click the OK button or press the Enter key.
4. The Windows Registry Editor opens. In the left window pane, double-click the HKEY_CLASSES_ROOT registry key. If you can't find it, do the following:
    a. In the left window pane of the Registry Editor, scroll to the top.
    b. If any of the HKEY registry keys are open — as indicated by a minus sign (-) on their left side — then close them by clicking that minus sign. When a registry key is properly closed, it has a plus sign (+) next to it.
    c. Repeat this process for the remaining HKEY registry keys until the only things visible in the left window pane are the five HKEY keys (see Figure 8-3).
    d. Double-click the HKEY_CLASSES_ROOT registry key.

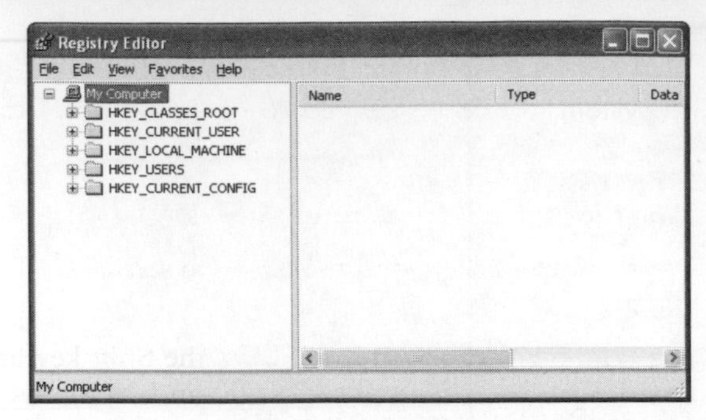

Figure 8-3

5. A long list of registry keys appears. Scroll down the list until you find Directory, and then double-click it. You may have difficulty locating this key because it is buried between other keys that have long names. On most Windows XP computers, the Directory key is located between the DirectFrame key and the DirectPlay key.
6. Underneath Directory, single-click the Shell registry key (see Figure 8-4).

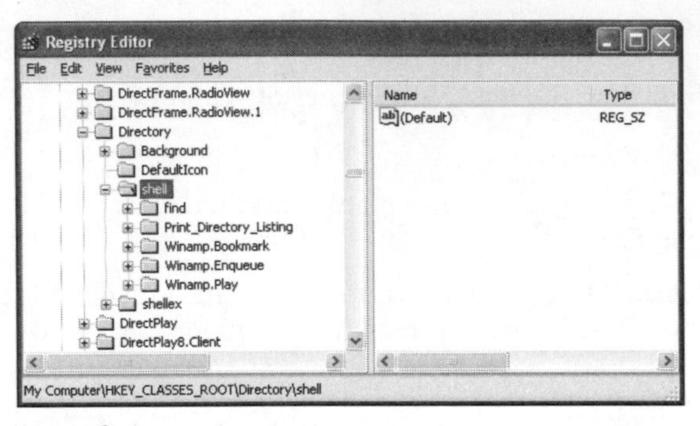

Figure 8-4

7. Right-click the Default registry value in the right window pane and select Modify.
8. A window opens. Under the Value Data heading, delete any words you find. Type **none** in their place.
9. Click the OK button.
10. Exit the Registry Editor by clicking the X button in the upper-right corner.

Rename Several Files at Once

If you want to give new names to a group of files that share a common theme—such as a collection of digital photos taken during a vacation—you can save yourself time and finger cramps by renaming them all at once (known as a "batch rename"). Follow these steps:

Note

A batch rename can be done in only one folder at a time. Also, be careful not to accidentally rename any critical system files. Doing so could cause Windows to malfunction.

1. Select the files you want to rename using one of the following methods:
   - Simultaneously press the Ctrl key and the A key to select all of the files in a folder.
   - Click the first item in a list, and then hold down the Shift key and click the last item in the list. This causes the first and last items and any between them to be highlighted.
   - Hold down the Ctrl key on your keyboard while clicking each individual item you want to select.
2. Right-click the file you want to go first in the newly renamed series.
3. Select Rename.
4. Type a name for the first file in the series, and then press the Enter key.
5. All of your selected files are given this new name, followed by a number that distinguishes them from one another. For example, if you renamed the first file Geeks On Call, then the rest of the files would be named Geeks On Call 1, Geeks On Call 2, Geeks On Call 3, and so on.
6. If you are unhappy with the new names, you can restore the original ones by simultaneously pressing the Ctrl and Z keys on your keyboard. Each time you use this keyboard shortcut, only one file reverts to its original name. That means you must use this shortcut numerous times to restore all of the names.

Automatically Insert the Date and Time into a Text File

If you use the Windows Notepad on a regular basis to keep a personal journal or to jot down spur-of-the-moment thoughts, you can create a special text file that automatically inserts the current time and date whenever it is opened. Here's how:

1. Click the Start button in the lower-left corner of Windows.
2. Click All Programs.
3. Select Accessories.
4. Click Notepad.
5. After Notepad opens, type **.LOG** (be sure to use all capital letters and include the period before them—see Figure 8-5).

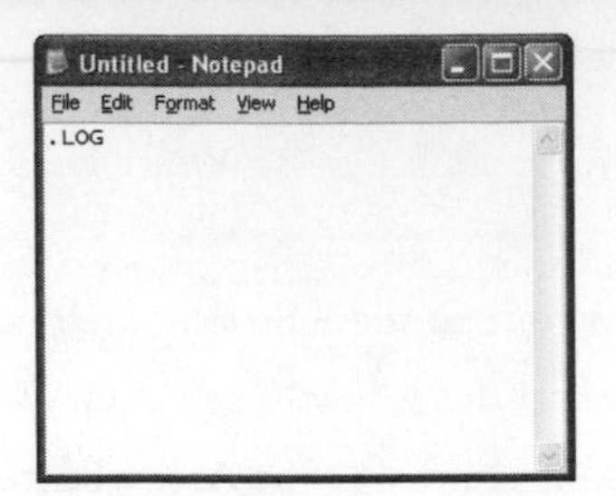

Figure 8-5

6. Click the File drop-down menu located in the upper-left corner of Notepad.
7. Select Save.
8. A window opens. In the File Name box, type a name that will help you identify the file (such as My Journal or Notes).
9. Select a location to save the file by clicking the Save In drop-down menu located at the top of this window.
10. Click the Save button located in the lower-right corner.
11. You are returned to the main Notepad screen. To exit, click the X button in the upper-right corner.

Each time you open this special text file, the day and time will be automatically inserted.

Edit the Send To Menu

Windows XP has a time-saving technique that enables you to right-click a file, select Send To, and click the name of a program, which causes that file to open inside of your chosen program. By default, Windows XP only has a few programs listed in the Send To menu, but you can easily add more and customize this menu to your liking. Follow these steps:

1. Locate a folder or program you frequently use, and then create a desktop shortcut to it. For more information on this process, please refer to "Create Desktop Shortcuts for Folders" and "Create Desktop Shortcuts for Windows Programs" in Chapter 7.
2. Right-click the shortcut you just created, and then select Cut.
3. Double-click the My Computer icon on your desktop. If this icon is not available, click the Start button in the lower-left corner of Windows and click My Computer. If you can't find the My Computer icon anywhere, do the following:
    a. Right-click in the empty space on your desktop.
    b. Select Properties.

  c. A window opens. Click the Desktop tab.
  d. Click the Customize Desktop button near the bottom of the window.
  e. Another window opens. On the General tab, beneath Desktop Icons, place a checkmark in the My Computer box.
  f. Click the OK button.
  g. You are returned to the previous screen. Click the Apply button.
  h. Click the OK button.
  i. The My Computer icon appears on your desktop. Double-click it.

4. A window opens. Double-click the icon for your C: drive (unless you installed Windows in a different location, in which case you would double-click that drive letter).
5. Double-click the Documents and Settings folder.
6. Double-click the folder containing the name of your Windows account. For example, if your account is named Bob, then double-click the Bob folder.
7. Inside your Windows account folder, click the Tools drop-down menu.
8. Select Folder Options.
9. A window opens. Click the View tab.
10. Under the Advanced Settings heading, scroll down and click the Show Hidden Files and Folders button.
11. Click the Apply button.
12. Click the OK button.
13. Back inside your Windows account folder, several hidden folders appear. Double-click the SendTo folder.
14. Inside the SendTo folder, right-click in the empty space and select Paste. Your new desktop shortcut appears.
15. If necessary, repeat this process to paste more shortcuts in the SendTo folder.
16. Click the Tools drop down menu.
17. Select Folder Options.
18. A window opens. Click the View tab.
19. Under the Advanced Settings heading, scroll down and click the Do Not Show Hidden Files and Folders button.
20. Click the Apply button.
21. Click the OK button.

22. Exit the SendTo folder by clicking the X button in the upper-right corner.
23. From now on, whenever you right-click a file or folder and select Send To, you will have the option to send a copy of it to one of the locations you added.

Create Audio and Visual Warnings for Caps Lock, Num Lock, and Scroll Lock

If you are like many computer users who never learned how to type properly, you probably spend more time looking at your keyboard than looking at the computer screen. This could be problematic, especially if you accidentally press the Caps Lock key and type several sentences in all capital letters before you notice your mistake. To prevent this, you can tweak Windows to notify you whenever you press the Caps Lock, Numbers Lock, or Scroll Lock keys. Here's how:

1. Click the Start button in the lower-left corner of Windows.
2. Click the Control Panel. (If you don't see this option, your Start menu is in classic mode. In that case, click Settings, and then select the Control Panel.)
3. Click Accessibility Options. If your Control Panel is in classic view, proceed to Step 4. If your Control Panel is in category view, the Pick a Task screen appears. Toward the bottom of this screen, click the Accessibility Options icon.
4. A window opens. Click the Keyboard tab.
5. Under the ToggleKeys heading, put a checkmark in the Use ToggleKeys box.
6. Click the Sound tab.
7. Under the SoundSentry heading, put a checkmark in the Use SoundSentry box.
8. Use the Choose the Visual Warning drop-down menu to select your preferred method of visual warning: Flash the active caption bar, Flash the active window, or Flash the desktop.
9. Click the Apply button.
10. Click the OK button.

Create a Screensaver Shortcut

Another time-saving technique is to create a desktop shortcut to your favorite screensaver. That way, if you need to step away from your computer, you can use the shortcut to launch the screensaver immediately. Follow these steps:

1. Click the Start button in the lower-left corner of Windows.
2. Select Search.

3. The Windows Search Companion opens. If the Search Companion is in standard mode, click the words in the left window pane that say All files and folders. If your Search Companion is in advanced mode, proceed to the next step.
4. In the All or Part of the File Name box, type ***.scr** (see Figure 8-6).

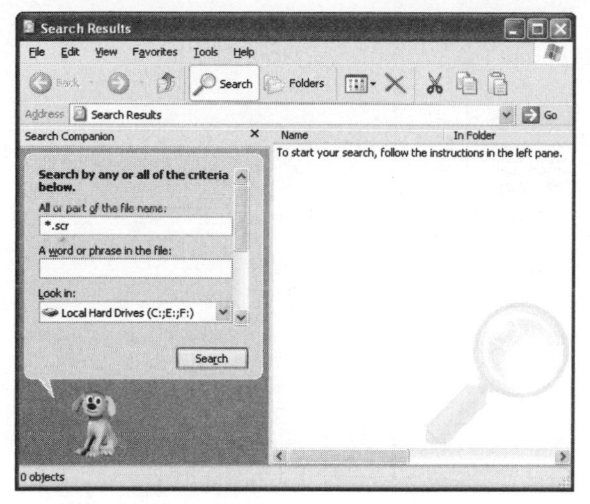

Figure 8-6

5. In the Look In drop-down menu, select Local Hard Drives.
6. Click the Search button.

   The Search Companion looks for screensavers in all of the folders on your computer. Depending on the speed of your computer, this process could take a few minutes. When the search is complete, a vertical list of your screensavers appears.
7. Decide which screensaver will receive a shortcut. If you are unsure, view a sample of each one by right-clicking it and selecting Test (but hold your mouse still, because any movement will prevent the screensaver from playing).
8. Once you have selected a screensaver, right-click it and select Create Shortcut.
9. A message will alert you that "Windows Cannot Create a Shortcut Here. Do You Want the Shortcut to Be Placed on the Desktop Instead?" Click the Yes button.
10. Close the Search Companion by clicking the X button in the upper-right corner.
11. Go to your desktop and find the screensaver shortcut. From now on, you can quickly launch the screensaver by double-clicking its shortcut.
12. If you want to use your keyboard to start the screensaver, right-click the new shortcut and select Properties.

13. A window opens. In the center of it is a box labeled Shortcut Key, next to which is the word None. Click this word, then type a letter (it can be any letter you choose). The word None disappears, and in its place appears Ctrl + Alt + *your letter* (see Figure 8-7). In this example, the letter *S* was used, so the shortcut Ctrl + Alt + S appears.

Figure 8-7

14. Click the Apply button.
15. Click the OK button.
16. From now on, you can activate the screensaver from your keyboard by simultaneously pressing the Ctrl, Alt, and *your letter* keys.

Use Keyboard Shortcuts

One of the best time-saving features of Windows is also one of the least known: keyboard shortcuts. By pressing a few buttons on your keyboard, you can accomplish the same tasks that normally would take much longer with a mouse. The following tables list the Windows and Internet Explorer keyboard shortcuts.

Windows Shortcuts

Keyboard Combination	*Result*
Alt + E	Opens the Edit menu
Alt + Enter	Opens the Properties window
Alt + F	Opens the File menu
Alt + F4	Closes the current program
Alt + Print Screen	Takes a screen shot of the current window or program
Alt + Tab	Switches between the programs currently in use

Keyboard Combination	*Result*
Ctrl + A	Selects all text
Ctrl + C	Copies the selected object
Ctrl + End	Jumps to the end of the current document
Ctrl + Esc	Opens the Start menu
Ctrl + F4	Closes the current program
Ctrl + Home	Jumps to the beginning of the current document
Ctrl + Insert	Copies the selected object
Ctrl + left arrow	Moves to the left one word
Ctrl + right arrow	Moves to the right one word
Ctrl + V	Pastes the selected object
Ctrl + X	Cuts the selected object
Ctrl + the "+" key	Perfectly resizes the width of Explorer columns
End	Jumps to the end of the current line
F1	Opens the Help menu
F2	Renames the selected icon
F3	Launches the Search Companion in a folder or on the desktop
F4	Accesses the Address Bar in a folder or window
F5	Refreshes the contents of a folder or window
Home	Jumps to the beginning of the current line
Shift + Delete	Permanently deletes files (bypasses the Recycle Bin)
Shift + End	Highlights text from the current position to the end of the line
Shift + F10	Substitutes for a right-click
Shift + Home	Highlights text from the current position to the beginning of the line
Shift + Insert	Pastes the selected object
Shift while inserting	Prevents the CD player from playing an audio CD

Shortcuts for Keyboards with a "Windows" Key (Resembling a Flag)

Keyboard Combination	*Result*
Windows Key + E	Opens Windows Explorer
Windows Key + F	Launches the Windows Search Companion

continued

Shortcuts for Keyboards with a "Windows" Key (Resembling a Flag) *continued*

Keyboard Combination	*Result*
Windows Key + F1	Opens the Help and Support Center
Windows Key + L	Locks down Windows
Windows Key + M	Minimizes all windows and shows the desktop
Windows Key + M + Shift	Undoes the minimize
Windows Key +	Opens the System Properties window Pause/Break key
Windows Key + R	Opens the Run window
Windows Key + U	Launches the Utility Manager

Internet Explorer Shortcuts

Keyboard Combination	*Result*
Alt + left arrow	Returns to the previous Web page
Alt + right arrow	Moves forward one Web page
Ctrl + N	Opens a new browser window
Ctrl + P	Prints the current Web page
Ctrl + Enter	Fills in a Web address. For example, if you type `geeksoncall` in the address bar then press Ctrl + Enter, you will get `http://www.geeksoncall.com`
Esc	Halts the current Web page from loading
F5	Refreshes the current Web page
F11	Displays a Web page in full-screen mode. To exit this mode, press F11 again.
Spacebar	Moves down one Web page at a time
Spacebar + Shift	Moves up one Web page at a time

Use WordPad

Windows XP has a word-processing program known as WordPad that allows you to create basic text documents. Although WordPad does not have the professional features found in a top-of-the-line word-processing program (like Microsoft Word), it does have significant advantages over its bare-bones brother, Notepad. For that reason, many people prefer WordPad for creating memos, jotting down quick notes, or making simple to-do lists. Here is where you can find it:

1. Click the Start button in the lower-left corner of Windows.
2. Click All Programs.
3. Select Accessories.
4. Click WordPad.
5. A quick and convenient way to access WordPad is to create a desktop shortcut to it.
    a. Right-click the WordPad icon.
    b. Select Send To.
    c. Select Desktop (create shortcut).

Upgrade WordPad

If you want a word-processing program that is more advanced than WordPad but doesn't have the price tag of Microsoft Word, consider downloading a WordPad-replacement program. Here are two popular choices (both of which are free):

- Jarte (`http://www.jarte.com`)
- MetaPad (`http://welcome.to/metapad`)

Update Your Video Card Drivers

If your computer is a few years old and you notice that it seems to "hiccup" now and again while watching DVD movies, playing video games, or doing other graphics-intensive activities, then you might benefit from upgrading the drivers for your video card. *Drivers* are a set of instructions that tell your computer how it should interact with a piece of hardware like a video card. Manufacturers often release new versions of their drivers on a regular basis, so the chances are good that you will be able to download new ones. Here's how:

1. First, you need to determine the age and version of your current video-card drivers. Click the Start button in the lower-left corner of Windows.
2. Click the Control Panel. (If you don't see this option, your Start menu is in classic mode. In that case, click Settings, and then select the Control Panel.)
3. If the Control Panel is in category view, click the Performance and Maintenance category, and then click the System icon. If the Control Panel is in classic view, simply double-click the System icon.
4. A window opens. Click the Hardware tab.
5. Click the Device Manager button.

6. Another window opens. Double-click Display Adapters (see Figure 8-8).

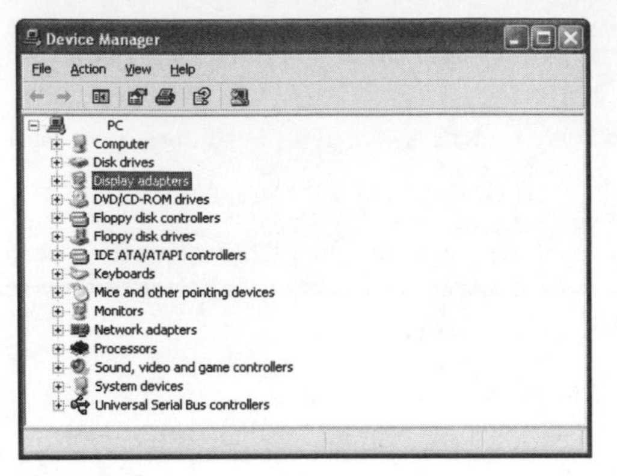

Figure 8-8

7. The name of your video card is displayed. Double-click it.
8. A new window opens. Click the Driver tab.
9. At the top of this window is the name of your video card. Below it are listed three important categories: Driver Provider, Driver Date, and Driver Version. Grab a pen and paper and write down all of this information.
10. Exit this window by clicking the Cancel button.
11. You are returned to the previous window. Exit it by clicking the X button in the upper-right corner.
12. Connect to the Internet.
13. Use your Web browser to visit an Internet search engine like Yahoo!, MSN, or Google. Do a search on the name of your video card's manufacturer. After finding a link to the manufacturer's website, click it.
14. At the site, look for a link with one of the following names: Drivers, Software, Downloads, Support, or Customer Service.
15. Once you have found the link, you are taken to a section of the website that allows you to search for graphics or video-card drivers. Search only for those designed for Windows XP. To find the appropriate drivers for your specific video card, refer to the information you jotted down, particularly the name of your card and the driver version. Be careful not to accidentally download drivers that have an older, lower version number, because this could cause your video card to have worse problems.
16. After you locate the most recent drivers for your video card, download their installation program to your computer. If you followed the "Easily Locate Your Downloads" 5-minute fix in Chapter 3 and created a separate Downloads folder on your computer, then save the installation program there.

17. Disconnect from the Internet, and then locate the installation program and double-click it. The installation of your new drivers begins. Follow the on-screen instructions.
18. When the installation is complete, you are asked to restart your computer.

Get the Best Picture

If your computer is fairly new, or if you recently installed a new video card, then your system is probably capable of viewing images at the highest quality settings. To do so, follow these steps:

1. Right-click the My Computer icon on your desktop. If this icon is not available, then click the Start button in the lower-left corner of Windows and right-click My Computer. If you can't find the My Computer icon anywhere, do the following:
   a. Right-click in the empty space on your desktop.
   b. Select Properties.
   c. A window opens. Click the Desktop tab.
   d. Near the bottom of the window, click the Customize Desktop button.
   e. Another window opens. On the General tab, beneath Desktop Icons, place a checkmark in the My Computer box.
   f. Click the OK button.
   g. You are returned to the previous screen. Click the Apply button.
   h. Click the OK button.
   i. The My Computer icon appears on your desktop. Double-click it.
2. Select Properties.
3. A window opens. Click the Advanced tab.
4. Under the Performance heading, click the Settings button.
5. Another window opens. Under the Visual Effects tab, click the Adjust for Best Appearance button.
6. Click the Apply button.
7. Click the OK button.
8. Return to your desktop and right-click its empty space.
9. Select Properties.
10. A window opens. Click the Settings tab.
11. Under the Color Quality heading, it should say Highest (32 Bit). If it has a lower number, click the drop down menu and select Highest (32 Bit).

12. Click the Advanced button located near the lower-right corner of this window.
13. A new window opens. Click the Monitor tab.
14. Under the Monitor Settings heading, click the Screen Refresh Rate drop-down menu. If your monitor permits, select a high refresh like 72 Hertz, 75 Hertz, or more.
15. Click the Apply button.
16. Click the OK button.
17. If your eyes are bothered by the highest refresh rate, try the next highest one. Test each rate until you find one that feels comfortable and reduces eyestrain.

Install PowerToys

Give Windows XP extra oomph by installing special add-ins known as PowerToys. Developed by Microsoft, these programs are designed to enhance the existing features of Windows or add new ones. Each PowerToy is available free of charge on Microsoft's website: `http://www.microsoft.com/windowsxp/downloads/powertoys/xppowertoys.mspx`.

Note

Microsoft does not offer technical support for the PowerToys, so if you run into problems when using one of them, either call a certified computer professional like Geeks On Call or uninstall that particular PowerToy. Also, Microsoft warns that if you previously installed any PowerToys prior to April 23, 2002, you must uninstall the old PowerToys before installing the new versions.

The PowerToys programs include the following:

- **Tweak UI:** The gem of the PowerToys collection is this extraordinary program that provides advanced options for changing or tweaking settings in Windows and Internet Explorer. It also enables you to customize features that were previously inaccessible.
- **RAW Image Thumbnailer and Viewer:** By installing this PowerToy, you can view uncompressed photos in the RAW format taken directly from a digital camera.
- **HTML Slide Show Wizard:** With this PowerToy, you can view your digital photos in a special Internet-friendly slide show.
- **CD Slide Show Generator:** If you have digital photos stored on a CD-ROM, you can view them as a slide show thanks to this PowerToy.
- **Power Calculator:** This powerful digital calculator offers numerous features not found in the standard Windows calculator, such as graphs and conversions.

- **Image Resizer:** Thanks to this PowerToy, you can change the size of a picture by right-clicking it with your mouse.
- **Virtual Desktop Manager:** Instead of using only one Windows desktop, this PowerToy enables you to have up to four "virtual" desktops open at one time, each of which can have its own customized appearance, folders, and programs.
- **Taskbar Magnifier:** This handy PowerToy enables you to magnify areas of your screen.
- **Webcam Timershot:** If your computer has an Internet camera, you can use it to take pictures at scheduled times (such as every few minutes or every few hours).
- **ClearType Tuner:** If you use a laptop computer, or if you have an LCD monitor for your desktop computer, you may benefit from a special font known as ClearType that was designed to make words easier to read on those kinds of screens.

Note

ClearType should not be used on computers with traditional monitors, because it could make words appear blurry.

9

5-Minute Fixes

FAST FIXES FOR A SLOW COMPUTER

Another common problem that Windows XP users have is a slow or sluggish system. If your programs take an unusually long time to open, or if using XP feels like running barefoot through a puddle of Super Glue, then try the 5-minute fixes in this chapter.

Do It Yourself

Remove spyware

Corral a CPU hog

Defragment your hard drive

Slim down your hard drive

Add more memory

Remove Spyware

Spyware is a general term describing dangerous programs that sneak into your computer by tricking you into installing them or by hiding in other programs you install. One of the most noticeable symptoms of spyware infection is a computer that suddenly acts strangely and runs unusually slow. If you think you have a spyware problem, follow these steps:

1. Connect to the Internet.
2. Download two different spyware-removal programs. Some popular brands include:
   - Ad-Aware Free Version (`http://www.lavasoftusa.com`)
   - Spybot Search and Destroy (`http://www.safer-networking.org`)
   - Spy Sweeper (`http://www.webroot.com`)
   - eTrust PestPatrol (`http://www.ca.com`)
   - McAfee AntiSpyware (`http://www.mcafee.com`)
3. Disconnect from the Internet.
4. Uninstall all file-sharing programs like Kazaa, BitTorrent, Limewire, or Bearshare that are used for trading pirated MP3 files or movies. If you do not

eliminate these programs, they could reinstall any spyware you remove. To uninstall a program, follow these steps:

a. Click the Start button in the lower-left corner of Windows.
b. Click the Control Panel. (If you don't see this option, your start menu is in classic mode. In that case, click Settings, and then select the Control Panel.)
c. Double-click Add or Remove Programs.
d. A window opens. Scroll down the list until you see the name of a file-sharing program.
e. Click the name of the file-sharing program, and then click the button on its right labeled Remove.

5. Install one of the antispyware programs you just downloaded. If you downloaded Ad-Aware, then install it first.
6. Connect to the Internet.
7. Open the antispyware program, and then update it (often referred to as updating its "definitions"). This ensures that it is capable of removing the newest spyware threats.
8. Use the antispyware program to scan your *entire* computer. If it finds any spyware, make sure it removes or "quarantines" each piece.
9. If the antispyware program asks you to reboot your computer so it can properly remove stubborn pieces of spyware, then follow its instructions. Even if you are not asked to reboot, it is still a good idea.
10. When you return to Windows, install your second antispyware program.
11. Connect to the Internet.
12. Open the second antispyware program, and then update it.
13. Use the second antispyware program to scan your *entire* computer. If it finds any spyware, make sure it removes or quarantines each piece.
14. If one of your antispyware programs allows you to turn on "shields" to protect Windows from future infections, then do so.
15. If your computer still acts strangely, it might be infected with a different digital threat such as a virus, worm, or Trojan horse. Consider using antivirus software to scan for those threats.
16. If your computer still has problems, consult a certified computer professional like Geeks On Call.

Corral a CPU Hog

Sometimes, for no apparent reason, a program can be thrown out of whack and develop a glitch that causes it to chew up most of your computer's resources (referred to as "hogging the CPU"). Typically this happens when a computer boots up, but occasionally it can happen during the middle of a regular Windows session. To determine whether or not a program is hogging your CPU, you must check the CPU Usage Meter, like this:

1. Simultaneously press the Ctrl, Alt, and Delete keys, which will open the Windows Task Manager. (However, if your version of Windows is configured differently, you might see a Windows Security box. In that case, simply click the Task Manager button.)
2. A window opens. Click the Performance tab.
3. On the left side of this window is a CPU Usage digital meter (see Figure 9-1). If it reads anywhere between 90 and 100 percent, then you've got a hog on your hands.

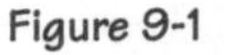

Figure 9-1

4. Click the Processes tab.
5. In the CPU column, look for the program that has a CPU usage of 90 or more. If necessary, use the scroll bar on the right to scroll down through the entire list until you find the culprit.
6. Click the name of the CPU hog.

Warning

Do not click on System Idle Process—even if it has a high number—because this is an essential Windows function that must not be touched.

7. Click the End Process button located near the bottom of this window.
8. Return to the Performance tab to verify that the CPU hog has been shut down and that your CPU usage has returned to a low number.

Defragment Your Hard Drive

The more you add or remove software, the more disorganized Windows becomes. To tidy up Windows and make it run faster and more efficiently, use a program called Disk Defragmenter. Follow these steps:

1. Close all open files and folders on your computer.
2. Temporarily disable your antivirus software as follows:
   a. Right-click the icon for your antivirus or antispyware program, which is usually located in the lower-right corner of Windows near the clock.
   b. Select the Close or Disable or Shut Down option.
3. Click the Start button in the lower-left corner of Windows.
4. Click All Programs.
5. Select Accessories.
6. Select System Tools.
7. Click Disk Defragmenter.
8. The Disk Defragmenter program opens. Near the top of this window, click the C: drive (unless you have Windows XP installed on a different drive, in which case you would click the letter for that drive).
9. Click the Analyze button located near the bottom of this window.
10. Your hard drive is scanned to determine whether or not it needs to be defragmented. If a message says "You should defragment this volume," then click the Defragment button (see Figure 9-2). The process will begin immediately and will probably take 30 to 60 minutes to complete (or more if you have a very slow computer). For the best results, do not use your computer until the defragmentation has finished.

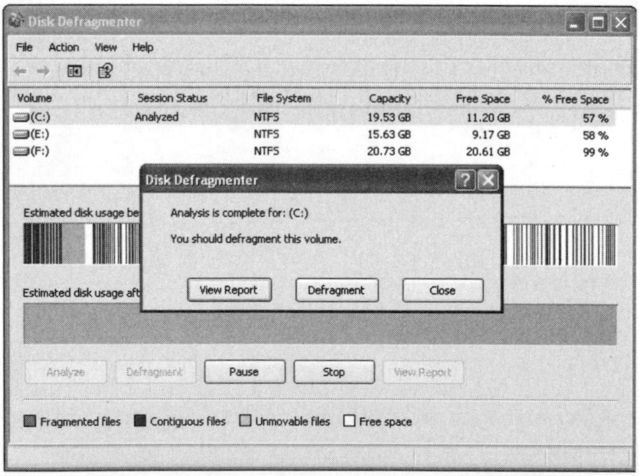

Figure 9-2

11. A message pops up to inform you that the defragmentation is complete. To read a detailed report about what occurred, click the View Report button. If you are not interested in seeing this report, simply click the Close button.
12. Turn on your antivirus software by right-clicking its icon near the Windows clock and selecting Enable or Restore. If the antivirus' icon is not there, then you must manually restart the program by doing the following:
    a. Click the Start button in the lower-left corner of Windows.
    b. Click All Programs.
    c. Select the folder containing the name of your antivirus software. For example, if you use Norton AntiVirus, then select the Norton AntiVirus folder.
    d. Click the shortcut to launch the program.

Slim Down Your Hard Drive

With most hard drives, the fuller they become, the slower they are. If your hard drive is stuffed to the brim with files and programs, you would benefit from transferring much of that data to a secondary hard drive (either an internal or external model will work fine). If you are unsure how to add another hard drive to your computer, consult a certified computer professional like Geeks On Call.

Add More Memory

If your computer constantly feels like a turtle walking through molasses, you probably need more system memory, also referred to as RAM. To operate efficiently, Windows XP needs at least 256 megabytes of RAM (but preferably more). Here is how you can find out how much you currently have:

1. Right-click the My Computer icon on your desktop. If this icon is not available, then click the Start button in the lower-left corner of Windows and right-click My Computer. If you can't find the My Computer icon anywhere, do the following:
    a. Right-click in the empty space on your desktop.
    b. Select Properties.
    c. A window opens. Click the Desktop tab.
    d. Click the Customize Desktop button near the bottom of the window.
    e. Another window opens. On the General tab, beneath Desktop Icons, place a checkmark in the My Computer box.
    f. Click the OK button.

g. You are returned to the previous screen. Click the Apply button.

h. Click the OK button.

i. The My Computer icon appears on your desktop. Double-click it.

2. Select Properties.

3. A window opens. Under the General tab, look for Computer. Beneath it, you should see the name of your CPU as well as your total amount of system RAM. If this number is less than 256 MB, you would benefit from a RAM upgrade. Consult a certified computer professional like Geeks On Call.

10

TURBOCHARGE XP

5-Minute Fixes™

In the 1990s television sitcom *Home Improvement*, a character named Tim Taylor was obsessed with turbocharging everyday devices like vacuums or lawn mowers. His motto: "More Power!" You too can add more power to Windows XP and make it faster by following the 5-minute fixes in this chapter.

Adjust Visuals for Best Performance

Windows XP contains many visual options and enhancements designed to make it more eye catching. If your computer is several years old — or if it has less than 256 megabytes of RAM — then you should disable these features to make your system more efficient. Here's how:

1. Right-click the My Computer icon on your desktop. If this icon is not available, click the Start button in the lower-left corner of Windows and right-click My Computer. If you can't find the My Computer icon anywhere, do the following:
   a. Right-click in the empty space on your desktop.
   b. Select Properties.
   c. A window opens. Click the Desktop tab.
   d. Near the bottom of the window, click the Customize Desktop button.
   e. Another window opens. On the General tab, beneath Desktop Icons, place a checkmark in the My Computer box.
   f. Click the OK button.
   g. You are returned to the previous screen. Click the Apply button.
   h. Click the OK button.
   i. The My Computer icon appears on your desktop. Double-click it.
2. Select Properties.
3. A window opens. Click the Advanced tab.

Do It Yourself

Adjust visuals for best performance

Start Windows faster

Disable qttask

Disable unneeded services

Reduce your fonts

Dust your computer

Get rid of unused programs

Cut out the FAT32

Disable the Indexing service

Transfer data at high speeds

Adjust virtual memory

4. Under the Performance heading, click the Settings button.
5. Another window opens. Under the Visual Effects tab, click the Adjust for Best Performance button.
6. Click the Apply button.
7. Click the OK button.

Start Windows Faster

One of the best ways to help your computer start more quickly is to reduce the number of programs that are loaded while Windows is "waking up." To tweak the startup, you must use a utility called msconfig, as follows:

1. Click the Start button in the lower-left corner of Windows.
2. Click Run.
3. A window opens. Type **msconfig** in the blank, and then click the OK button or press the Enter key.
4. The System Configuration Utility window opens. Click the Startup tab on the far right.
5. In the Startup Item column on the left is a list of programs with checkmarks next to them (see Figure 10-1). A checkmark indicates that the program is scheduled to launch each time Windows starts. To prevent a program from loading at startup, remove the checkmark from its box. Here are guidelines about which programs to allow or to disable:
    - Disable non-essential multimedia programs like qttask (which is part of the QuickTime software), realsched (which is part of the RealPlayer software), or Adobe Reader.
    - Allow common processes for Windows and Microsoft Office.
    - Allow programs related to your antivirus software, antispyware software, or firewall. For example, if you use the ZoneAlarm firewall and Spy Sweeper antispyware program, then you should allow the startup programs named zlclient and SpySweeper.
    - Allow programs related to your printer. For example, if you have an Epson printer, then allow the startup program named Epson Status Monitor.

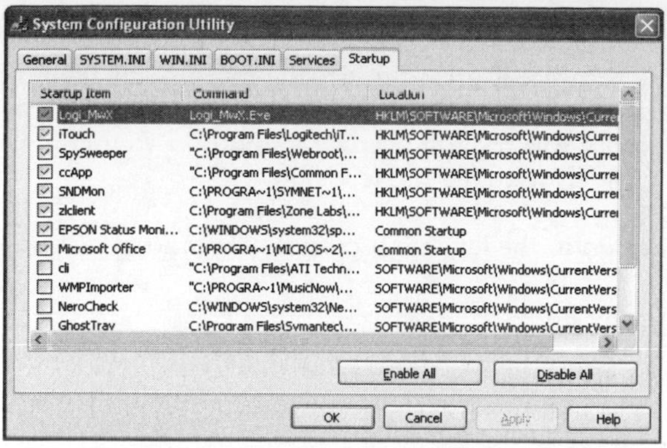

Figure 10-1

6. If you are uncertain about whether or not to disable a particular program, do the following:

   a. Write the program's name on a piece of paper.

   b. Connect to the Internet.

   c. In your Web browser, type **http://www.processlibrary.com** to visit the Process Library.

   d. Near the top of this website's main page is a Search for a Process search box. Type the name of your program into this box, and then click the Search Now button.

      You are taken to a Web page that explains what your program is used for and whether or not it is essential to your computer's performance.

7. When you have finished tweaking the System Configuration Utility, click the Apply button.

8. Click the OK button.

9. A message alerts you that you must restart your computer for the changes to take effect. Click the Restart button. Your computer automatically shuts down and reboots.

10. When you return to Windows, a message alerts you that you have just used the System Configuration Utility to change the way Windows starts. Put a checkmark in the box labeled "Don't show this message or launch the system configuration utility when Windows starts."

11. Click the OK button.

Disable qttask

Although the QuickTime software is great for viewing multimedia content on the Internet, it has an annoying habit of launching a program called qttask each time Windows starts. Because this program can be a drain on your computer's resources, you should consider disabling it. Here's how:

1. Click the Start button in the lower-left corner of Windows.
2. Click Run.
3. A window opens. Type **msconfig** in the blank, and then click the OK button or press the Enter key.
4. The System Configuration Utility window opens. Click the Startup tab on the far right.
5. In the Startup Item column on the left, remove the checkmark from the qttask box (see Figure 10-2).

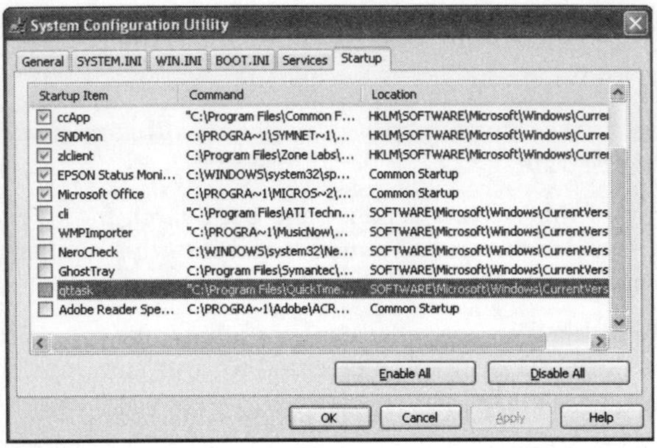

Figure 10-2

6. Click the Apply button.
7. Click the OK button.
8. A message alerts you that you must restart the computer for the changes to take effect. Click the Exit without Restart button.
9. Double-click the My Computer icon on your desktop. If this icon is not available, then click the Start button in the lower-left corner of Windows and click My Computer. If you can't find the My Computer icon anywhere, do the following:
   a. Right-click in the empty space on your desktop.
   b. Select Properties.
   c. A window opens. Click the Desktop tab.
   d. Click the Customize Desktop button near the bottom of the window.

e. Another window opens. On the General tab, beneath Desktop Icons, place a checkmark in the My Computer box.

f. Click the OK button.

g. You are returned to the previous screen. Click the Apply button.

h. Click the OK button.

i. The My Computer icon appears on your desktop. Double-click it.

10. A window opens. Double-click the icon for your C: drive (unless you installed Windows in a different location, in which case, double-click that drive letter).

11. Double-click the Program Files folder.

12. Double-click the QuickTime folder.

13. Find the qttask program, and then right-click it and select Rename.

14. Type a new name for the program, such as **qttask renamed**.

15. Shut down your computer and restart it.

16. When you return to Windows, a message alerts you that you have just used the System Configuration Utility to change the way Windows starts. Put a checkmark in the box labeled "Don't show this message or launch the system configuration utility when Windows starts."

17. Click the OK button.

Disable Unneeded Services

Another way to reduce the strain on an aging computer is to disable some non-essential Windows services. Follow these steps:

1. Click the Start button in the lower-left corner of Windows.

2. Click the Control Panel. (If you don't see this option, your Start menu is in classic mode. In that case, click Settings, and then select the Control Panel.)

3. If the Control Panel is in category view, click the Performance and Maintenance category, and then click the Administrative Tools icon. If the Control Panel is in classic view, simply double-click the Administrative Tools icon.

4. Double-click the Services icon.

5. A window opens. Using the scroll bar, scroll down until you see Alerter, and then double-click it.

6. Another window opens. Click the Startup Type drop-down menu, and then select Disabled (see Figure 10-3).

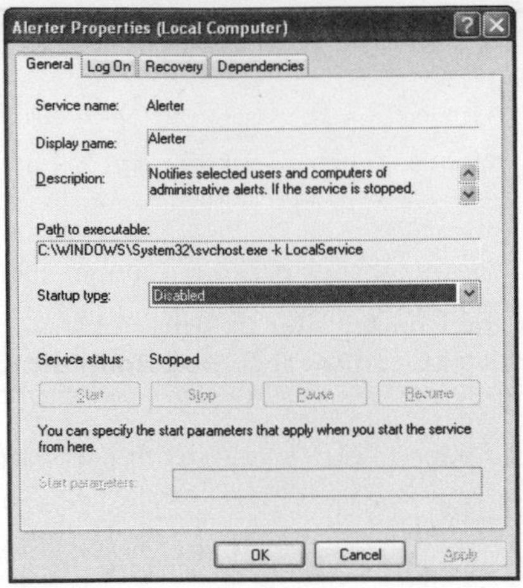

Figure 10-3

7. Click the Apply button.
8. Click the OK button.
9. Return to the Services window and repeat the previous steps to disable the following services:
   - **IMAPI CD-Burning COM Service:** This service controls the basic, no-frills CD-burning program built into Windows XP. If you currently use a separate CD-burning program like Nero Burning ROM, Easy Media Creator, or NTI CD-Maker, then you can disable the IMAPI service. Doing so should not affect your burning program, and might even make it faster. However, if problems arise, then simply return to this window and re-enable IMAPI.
   - **Indexing Service**
   - **MS Software Shadow Copy Provider:** If you have the Professional Edition of Windows XP and want to use its internal Backup program, then do not disable this service. Otherwise, this service is unnecessary.
   - **Volume Shadow Copy:** If you have the Professional Edition of Windows XP and want to use its internal backup program, then do not disable this service. Otherwise, this service is unnecessary.

Reduce Your Fonts

A *font* refers to the style and appearance of the words you type in a word-processor or similar program. A little-known fact about fonts is that having too many of them increases the time it takes for Windows to start. If you have a large collection of fonts but don't want to delete any, then do the following:

1. Double-click the My Computer icon on your desktop. If this icon is not available, then click the Start button in the lower-left corner of Windows and click My Computer. If you can't find the My Computer icon anywhere, do the following:
   a. Right-click in the empty space on your desktop.
   b. Select Properties.
   c. A window opens. Click the Desktop tab.
   d. Click the Customize Desktop button near the bottom of the window.
   e. Another window opens. On the General tab, beneath Desktop Icons, place a checkmark in the My Computer box.
   f. Click the OK button.
   g. You are returned to the previous screen. Click the Apply button.
   h. Click the OK button.
   i. The My Computer icon appears on your desktop. Double-click it.
2. A window opens. Double-click the icon for your C: drive (unless you installed Windows in a different location, in which case, double-click that drive letter).
3. Double-click the Windows folder.
4. You might see a message that says, "This folder contains files that keep your system working properly, so there is no need to modify its contents." If so, click the message below it that says, "Show files or Show the contents of this folder."
5. Double-click the Fonts folder.
6. Inside this folder, determine how many fonts you have by looking at the lower-left corner of the Status Bar. If you don't have the Status Bar enabled, then do the following:
   a. At the top of the folder, click the View drop-down menu.
   b. Click Status Bar.
   c. The status bar appears at the bottom of the folder.
7. If you have more than 300 fonts, browse through them and decide which ones you rarely use and can be moved to a different folder. To preview a font, double-click its name.
8. Hold down the Ctrl key while clicking the name of each font you want to move. This causes your selected fonts to become highlighted.
9. Click the Edit drop-down menu.
10. Select Copy.
11. Return to your C: drive, and then click the File drop-down menu.
12. Select New.

13. Select Folder.
14. A New Folder appears in your C: drive. Right-click it, and then select Rename.
15. Type a new name for the folder such as Fonts2 or Other Fonts.
16. Double-click the folder to open it.
17. Inside the folder, right-click the empty space and select Paste. Your selected fonts are pasted into the folder.
18. Return to your original Fonts folder and delete the fonts you just copied.
19. If you ever need to use one of the fonts you moved, do the following:
    a. Right-click the font, and then select Copy.
    b. Open your original Fonts folder.
    c. Click the Edit drop-down menu.
    d. Select Paste. The font is installed to its original location.

FYI

Another way to give your computer a speed boost is to install a fast hard drive or a cutting-edge video card. Both of these could breathe new life into an old PC.

Dust Your Computer

Did you know that a buildup of dust and debris inside your computer's case can lead to decreased performance or hardware damage? Protect your high-tech investment by dusting the inside of your computer each month. Follow these steps:

1. Purchase a can of compressed air. These can be found at office supply stores or large retailers like Wal-Mart.
2. Shut down your computer.
3. Unplug the computer's power cable from the electrical outlet on your wall or power strip. This is critical to protect you from dangerous electrical shocks.
4. Open the computer's case. Often this requires unscrewing an access panel located on the side or top of the case.
5. Before touching anything inside your computer, *ground* yourself by touching a metal piece of the case. This prevents static electricity from damaging your computer components.
6. Use the can of compressed air to blow out the dust and gunk. Be sure to get the dust that is trapped between your cables or sitting on your hard drive and CD/DVD drive.
7. When the inside of your computer is clean and clear, shut the case, and then plug the power cable back into an outlet.

Get Rid of Unused Programs

Are you a digital packrat? You might be if you have collected and installed countless programs and video games over the years but haven't gotten rid of the ones you no longer use. An easy way to clear room on your hard drive and to speed up Windows is to uninstall old programs that haven't seen the light of day in a long time. Here's how:

1. Click the Start button in the lower-left corner of Windows.
2. Click the Control Panel. (If you don't see this option, your Start menu is in classic mode. In that case, click Settings, and then select the Control Panel.)
3. Double-click Add or Remove Programs.
4. A window opens, containing a list of the programs installed on your computer. Scroll down the list and find the names of programs you no longer use.
5. Click the Remove button, and then follow the on-screen instructions to uninstall the software.
6. When the removal is complete, you may be asked to restart your computer.

Cut out the FAT32

The old versions of Windows (95, 98, ME) managed their files with a system known as FAT32. Although this same file system is available in Windows XP, it doesn't offer the improved performance and stability of a different file system called NTFS. If you want to maximize your computer's speed, cut out the FAT32 and convert your hard drives to NTFS.

Follow these steps to determine if you are using FAT32:

1. Double-click the My Computer icon on your desktop. If this icon is not available, then click the Start button in the lower-left corner of Windows and click My Computer. If you can't find the My Computer icon anywhere, do the following:
   a. Right-click in the empty space on your desktop.
   b. Select Properties.
   c. A window opens. Click the Desktop tab.
   d. Click the Customize Desktop button near the bottom of the window.
   e. Another window opens. On the General tab, beneath Desktop Icons, place a checkmark in the My Computer box.
   f. Click the OK button.
   g. You are returned to the previous screen. Click the Apply button.

h. Click the OK button.

i. The My Computer icon appears on your desktop. Double-click it.

2. A window opens. Right-click your C: drive (unless you installed Windows in a different location, in which case, double-click that drive letter).
3. Select Properties.
4. A window opens. Look for File System under the General tab. Next to it is either FAT32 or NTFS.

Follow these steps to convert to NTFS:

1. Back up all of the files on your computer, just in case something goes wrong during the conversion. For more information about backing up data, please refer to Chapter 5.
2. Click the Start button in the lower-left corner of Windows.
3. Click Run.
4. A window opens. Type **cmd** in the blank, and then click the OK button or press the Enter key.
5. Another window opens. At the command prompt, type **vol c:** and then press the Enter key.
6. The window displays the label of your C: drive (if it has one) as well as the Volume Serial Number. Write this information on a piece of paper.
7. At the command prompt, type **convert c: /fs:ntfs** (unless you want to convert another drive, in which case replace C: with a different drive letter followed by a colon). See Figure 10-4.

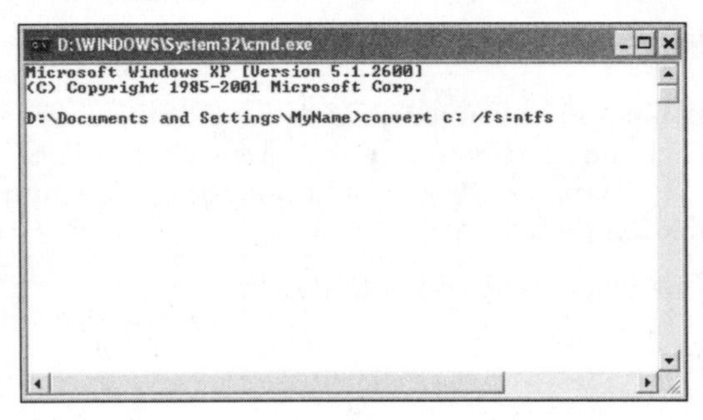

Figure 10-4

8. You are asked to type the label and Volume Serial Number for your drive, which you wrote down in Step 7 of this fix.
9. You are asked two additional questions. For each one, type **Y** then press the Enter key.

10. If you are converting a hard drive or partition that doesn't have Windows installed on it, then the conversion should begin immediately. If you are converting your main partition or hard drive on which Windows is installed, then you will likely need to shut down your computer and restart it before the conversion can begin.

11. After your computer boots into Windows, do not use it for a few minutes. This allows Windows to tidy up any loose ends left over from the conversion. After a few minutes have elapsed, you can use your computer again.

Disable the Indexing Service

Windows XP has a feature known as *Indexing* that is supposed to help the Search Companion find your files faster. Although there is some truth to this, it is also true that turning off Indexing can give a slight performance boost to an old or slow computer. To turn off Indexing:

1. Double-click the My Computer icon on your desktop. If this icon is not available, then click the Start button in the lower-left corner of Windows and click My Computer. If you can't find the My Computer icon anywhere, do the following:
    a. Right-click in the empty space on your desktop.
    b. Select Properties.
    c. A window opens. Click the Desktop tab.
    d. Click the Customize Desktop button near the bottom of the window.
    e. Another window opens. On the General tab, beneath Desktop Icons, place a checkmark in the My Computer box.
    f. Click the OK button.
    g. You are returned to the previous screen. Click the Apply button.
    h. Click the OK button.
    i. The My Computer icon appears on your desktop. Double-click it.
2. A window opens. Right-click your C: drive (unless you installed Windows in a different location, in which case, double-click that drive letter).
3. Select Properties.
4. A window opens. At the bottom of the General tab, remove the checkmark from the Allow Indexing Service to Index This Disk for Fast File Searching box.
5. Click the Apply button.
6. Click the OK button.
7. Repeat this process for your other hard drives.

Transfer Data at High Speeds

To maximize the performance of your hard drives or CD/DVD drives, Windows XP uses a high-speed method of transferring data known as DMA (direct memory access). If an error occurs and Windows cannot run a drive in this mode, it tries several times to re-enable DMA. If it is still unsuccessful, Windows switches the drive to PIO mode. If this occurs, you have to restore the DMA mode manually, as follows:

1. Click the Start button in the lower-left corner of Windows.
2. Click the Control Panel. (If you don't see this option, your Start menu is in classic mode. In that case, click Settings, and then select the Control Panel.)
3. If the Control Panel is in category view, click the Performance and Maintenance category, and then click the System icon. If the Control Panel is in classic view, simply double-click the System icon.
4. A window opens. Click the Hardware tab.
5. Click the Device Manager button.
6. Another window opens. Double-click IDE ATA/ATAPI Controllers.
7. Double-click Primary IDE Channel (see Figure 10-5).

Figure 10-5

8. A new window opens. Click the Advanced Settings tab.
9. Under the Device 0 and Device 1 headings, look for Current Transfer Mode. If the mode is listed as DMA, then your drive is already running at a high speed. If the mode is listed as PIO, then exit this window and return to the Device Manger.
10. Right-click the Primary IDE Channel.
11. Select Uninstall.
12. Repeat this process for the Secondary IDE Channel if it also has devices in PIO mode.

13. Shut down your computer and reboot.
14. When Windows reloads, it automatically reinstalls the deleted IDE channels. To find out if this reinstallation corrected the problem, return to the Device Manager.
15. Open the Primary IDE Channel and the Secondary IDE Channel, and see if DMA is listed as the current transfer mode. If the drive still says PIO, then you have to edit the Windows Registry.

Follow these steps to edit the Windows Registry:

1. Click the Start button in the lower-left corner of Windows.
2. Click Run.
3. A window opens. Type **regedit** in the blank, and then click the OK button or press the Enter key.
4. The Windows Registry Editor opens. In the left window pane, double-click the HKEY_LOCAL_MACHINE registry key. If you can't find it, do the following:
   a. In the left window pane of the Registry Editor, scroll to the top.
   b. If any of the HKEY registry keys are open — as indicated by a minus sign (-) on their left side — then close them by clicking that minus sign. When a registry key is properly closed, it has a plus sign (+) next to it.
   c. Repeat this process for the remaining HKEY registry keys until the only things visible in the left window pane are the five HKEY keys (see Figure 10-6).
   d. Double-click the HKEY_LOCAL_MACHINE registry key.

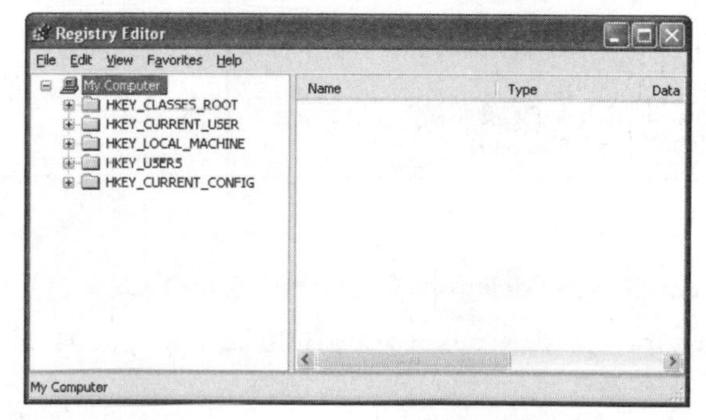

Figure 10-6

5. A new column of registry keys appears. Double-click System.
6. Another column of registry keys appears. Double-click CurrentControlSet.
7. Double-click the Control registry key.

8. A long list of registry keys appears. Double-click Class.

9. Another long list of registry keys appears. Scroll down and double-click {4D36E96A-E325-11CE-BFC1-08002BE10318}. See Figure 10-7.

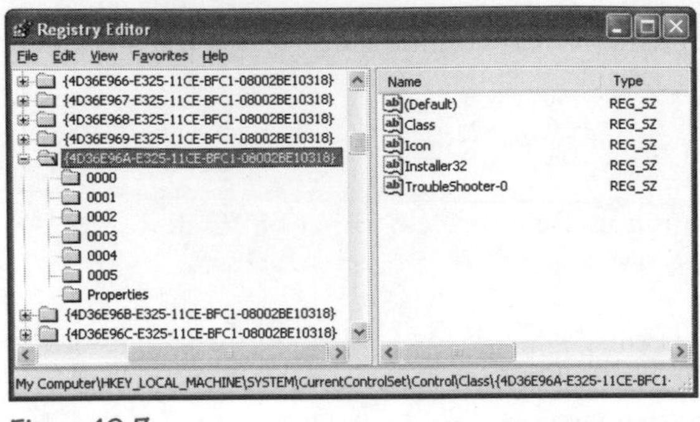

Figure 10-7

10. Several registry keys with sequential numbers are displayed: 0000, 0001, 0002, 0003, and so forth. Click 0000.

11. In the right window pane, look for MasterIdDataCheckSum and SlaveIdDataCheckSum (see Figure 10-8). If one or both of these are present, right-click them and select Delete.

Figure 10-8

12. You are asked to confirm the deletion. Click the Yes button.

13. Repeat this process for the registry keys 0001, 0002, 0003, 0004, and so on.

14. Exit the Registry Editor by clicking the X button in the upper-right corner.

15. Shut down your computer and restart it. When Windows reloads, it re-detects your hard drives and CD/DVD drives, which should cause them to be installed in DMA mode.

Adjust Virtual Memory

When Windows is under a heavy strain, it sometimes needs more system memory (RAM) than your computer currently has. In that case, it seeks help from a digital warehouse called Virtual Memory. No matter how little or how much RAM your computer has, you can adjust the settings of your Virtual Memory to ensure optimal performance. Here's how:

1. Right-click the My Computer icon on your desktop. If this icon is not available, click the Start button in the lower-left corner of Windows and right-click My Computer. If you can't find the My Computer icon anywhere, do the following:
    a. Right-click in the empty space on your desktop.
    b. Select Properties.
    c. A window opens. Click the Desktop tab.
    d. Near the bottom of the window, click the Customize Desktop button.
    e. Another window opens. On the General tab, beneath Desktop Icons, place a checkmark in the My Computer box.
    f. Click the OK button.
    g. You are returned to the previous screen. Click the Apply button.
    h. Click the OK button.
    i. The My Computer icon appears on your desktop. Right-click it.
2. Select Properties.
3. A window opens. Under the General tab, look for Computer. Beneath it, you should see the name of your CPU as well as your total amount of system RAM. Remember this number.
4. In the same window, click the Advanced tab.
5. Under the Performance heading, click the Settings button.
6. Another window opens. Click the Advanced tab.
7. Under the Virtual Memory heading, click the Change button.
8. A new window opens. Click the Custom Size button.
9. In the Initial Size (MB) and Maximum Size (MB)boxes, type a number based on the following formula:
    - If your computer has 128 MB of RAM, use 256 as the Initial Size and 512 as the Maximum Size.
    - If your computer has 256 MB of RAM, use 384 as the Initial Size and 768 as the Maximum Size.
    - If your computer has 512 MB of RAM, use 768 as the Initial Size and 1536 as the Maximum Size.

10. When you are finished adjusting the virtual memory, make your changes take hold by clicking the Set button.
11. Click the OK button.
12. You are returned to the previous window. Click the OK button.

PART III

HAVE FUN WITH XP

On a Lighter Note . . .

So far, the 5-minute fixes in this book have helped you to repair Windows XP or make it more powerful and useful. Now it's time to change the tune by showing you how to enjoy some of XP's fun and entertaining features, covered in Chapters 11 and 12.

11

CUSTOMIZE XP

5-Minute Fixes

Are you bored with the look of Windows XP? Are you tired of staring at the same, dull icons and desktop wallpaper or hearing the same, bland sound effects? Then give XP a complete overhaul by customizing its audio and visual features courtesy of the 5-minute fixes in this chapter.

Restore the Classic Windows Appearance

Some computer users consider the bright and colorful appearance of Windows XP to be irritating. Instead, they prefer the familiar blue and gray color scheme of older versions of Windows. If you share this perspective, it is easy to restore the classic Windows appearance. Just follow these steps:

1. Right-click the empty space on your desktop.
2. Select Properties.
3. A window opens. Click the Appearance tab.
4. In the middle of this window, under the Windows and Buttons heading, click the drop-down menu and select Windows Classic Style.
5. Click the Apply button.
6. Click the OK button.

Restore the Classic Windows Start Menu

Along with tweaking the color scheme of Windows XP, you can tweak the Start menu so that it too has the look and feel of an older version of Windows. Here's how:

1. Click the Start button in the lower-left corner of Windows.
2. Click the Control Panel. (If you don't see this option, your Start menu is in classic mode. In that case, click Settings, and then select the Control Panel.)

Do It Yourself

3. If the Control Panel is in category view, click the Appearance and Themes category, and then click the Taskbar and Start Menu icon. If the Control Panel is in classic view, simply double-click the Taskbar and Start Menu icon.
4. A window opens. Click the Start Menu tab.
5. Click the Classic Start Menu button.
6. Click the Apply button.
7. Click the OK button.

Add a Theme

To liven up your desktop, consider installing a *theme* (sometimes referred to as a suite), which is a collection of wallpaper, icons, cursors, and sounds that are centered around a common idea, place, movie, TV show, sports team, or any other topic. For example, a theme for the New England Patriots football team might include a wallpaper that shows images of the Patriots winning three Super Bowls in a four-year span, customized icons and cursors that look like football helmets, and football-related sound files that play whenever you do a common task like empty the Windows Recycle Bin.

The following 5-minute fixes tell you how to use various methods to add a theme.

Download Themes

There are plenty of sites on the Internet where you can find themes:

- Microsoft Plus (`http://www.microsoft.com/windows/plus/plushome.asp`)
- Theme World (`http://www.themeworld.com`)
- TopDownloads.net (`http://www.topdownloads.net/themes`)
- Look up the words Windows XP Themes on an Internet search engine like Yahoo, MSN, or Google.

Install a Theme

After downloading a theme, you typically have to unzip it (because most themes are stored in a "zip" file). This is easy to do thanks to Windows XP's built-in zip program. Follow these steps:

1. Locate the zip file you downloaded.
2. Right-click the file and select Extract All.
3. The Extraction Wizard opens. Click the Next button.

4. If you want to unzip the theme in the same folder it was downloaded to, click the Next button. If you want to unzip the theme in a different folder, click the Browse button, select a new location, and then click the OK button.

5. The theme will be extracted to your selected folder, which should only take a few seconds. When the process is complete, click the Finish button.

6. Once a theme is unzipped, you can install it. Right-click the empty space on your desktop.

7. Select Properties.

8. A window opens. Click the Themes tab.

9. Click the Theme drop-down menu, and then select Browse.

10. A window opens. In the center of it, find the folder where your unzipped theme is located, and then double-click the name of that folder. Generally the folder has the same name as the original zip file you downloaded. For example, if you downloaded a zipped theme named New England Patriots Theme, your unzipped files are located in a folder named New England Patriots Theme.

    Your new theme is installed, replacing your current one.

Change the Picture for Your Windows Account

To make your computing experience more fun and eye pleasing, you can customize your Windows XP account by changing the picture located beneath your account's name on the Start menu and the Welcome Screen. Windows comes pre-loaded with several dozen images to choose from, but if none of them catch your eye, you can easily use one of your own pictures. Here's how:

1. Click the Start button in the lower-left corner of Windows.

2. Click the Control Panel. (If you don't see this option, your Start menu is in classic mode. In that case, click Settings, and then select the Control Panel.)

3. Double-click User Accounts.

4. A window opens. Under the Pick a Task heading, click Change an Account.

5. Click the name of the account you want to change.

6. Click Change My Picture.

7. About two dozen pictures appear in the center of the window (see Figure 11 1). If you see one you like, click it, and then click the Change Picture button. The change occurs immediately.

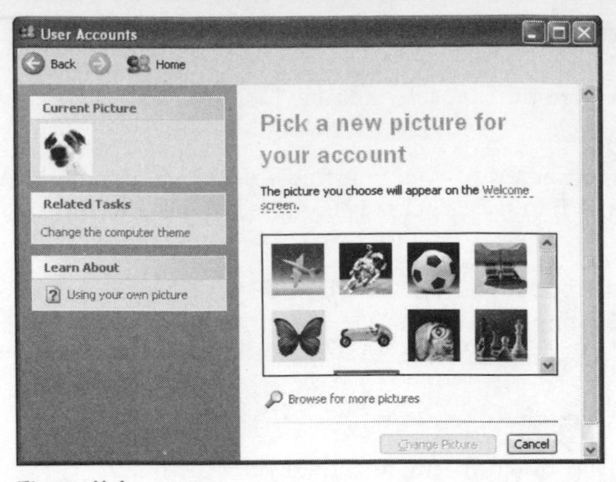

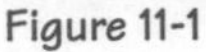
Figure 11-1

8. If you prefer to use one of your own pictures, do the following:
   a. In the center of the window, click Browse for More Pictures.
   b. A new window opens, displaying the contents of the My Pictures folder. If this is where you store your pictures and photos, then find one you like and double-click its name. The change occurs immediately.
   c. If you prefer to use a picture located in a different folder, click the Look In drop-down menu located at the top of this window.
   d. Browse through the drives and folders on your computer, and then double-click the name of a suitable picture or photo. The change occurs immediately.

Change the Desktop Wallpaper

The most noticeable way to customize the look of Windows is to change its desktop wallpaper. Doing this is like redecorating the inside of your home to make it an extension of your personality. If none of Windows' default images suit your tastes, you can always use a picture from the Internet or from a digital camera, like this:

1. Right-click the empty space on your desktop.
2. Select Properties.
3. The Display Properties window opens. Click the Desktop tab.
4. If you want to create wallpaper from one of your own pictures, proceed to Step 5. If you want to choose one of the pre-installed Windows wallpapers, then do the following:
   a. Under the heading labeled Background, click the name of a wallpaper to see a preview of it.
   b. When you find a wallpaper that suits you, click the Apply button.
   c. Click the OK button.

5. You can create custom wallpaper by selecting almost any picture or digital photo on your computer. Follow these steps:

   a. Click the Browse button located on the right side of this window.

   b. A new window opens, displaying the contents of the My Pictures folder. If this is where you store your pictures and photos, then find one that will make a suitable wallpaper and double-click its name.

   c. If you prefer to use a picture located in a different folder, click the Look In drop-down menu located at the top of this window.

   d. Browse through the drives and folders on your computer, and then double-click the name of a suitable picture or photo.

   e. You are returned to the Display Properties window, which displays a preview of your new wallpaper. If the preview screen indicates that your picture or photo will not fill the entire screen (see Figure 11-2), click the Position drop-down menu located on the right side of this window and select Stretch.

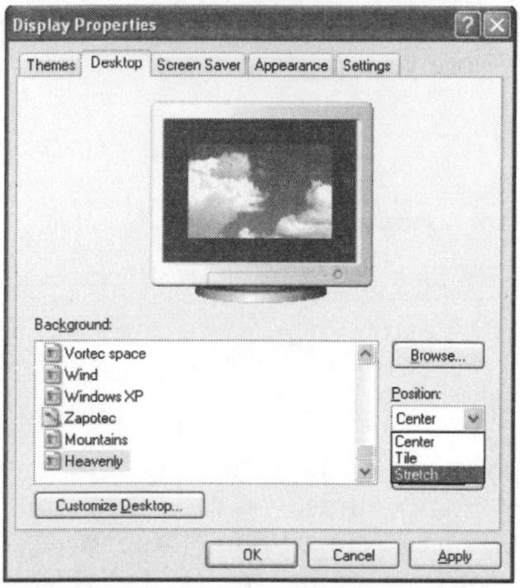

Figure 11-2

   f. Click the Apply button.

   g. Click the OK button.

Replace Your Icons

Are you tired of staring at the same, boring icons on your desktop? Does the drab, yellow color of Windows' folders annoy you? If so, you can inject even more of your personality into your computer by replacing your old, lifeless icons with new ones that are vibrant and entertaining. To do so, you need to download collections of icons or make your own, as described in the following sections.

Icon Collections

Numerous websites allow you to download collections of icons that are centered around a common theme. For example, you could pick icons that resemble the logos for professional sports teams or the characters from the *Scooby Doo* cartoons (see Figure 11-3). You'll be amazed by the hundreds of different categories available.

Figure 11-3

Here are some places to find free icons:

- Leo's Icon Archive (`http://www.iconarchive.com`)
- Look up the words Windows XP Icons on an Internet search engine like Yahoo, MSN, or Google.

Icon-Creation Software

For the ultimate in personalized icons, you can create your own from any picture or digital photo on your computer. For example, you can make icons that show your pet poodle Petunia, or the face of a beloved family member. (Wouldn't you just love to have an icon of your mother in-law staring at you day after day? Okay, just kidding.) Certainly the possibilities are endless. Although you might be able to find free icon-creation programs on the Internet, the best ones — which are also the easiest to use — must be purchased for a reasonable fee. Here are some popular titles (in no particular order):

- Microangelo (`http://www.microangelo.us`)
- IconForge (`http://www.cursorarts.com`)
- IconXP (`http://www.aha-soft.com/iconxp`)

Change Icons

After you have downloaded or created icons, follow these steps to replace your old icons with the new ones.

To change folder icons:

1. Right-click the folder you want to change.
2. Select Properties.
3. A window open. Click the Customize tab.
4. Near the bottom of this window, click the Change Icon button.
5. A new window opens. Click the Browse button.
6. Another window opens. To find the icon you want, click the Look In drop-down menu.
7. Browse through the drives and folders on your computer, and then double-click the name of a suitable icon.
8. Click the OK button.
9. You are returned to the original window. Click the Apply button.
10. Click the OK button.
11. To restore the original icon for a folder, do the following:
    a. Right-click the folder you want to change.
    b. Select Properties.
    c. A window opens. Click the Customize tab.
    d. Click the Change Icon button.
    e. A new window opens. Click the Restore Defaults button.
    f. You are returned to the original window. Click the Apply button.
    g. Click the OK button.

To change desktop shortcut icons:

1. Right-click the shortcut you want to change.
2. Select Properties.
3. A window opens. Click the Change Icon button.
4. A new window opens. Click the Browse button.
5. Another window opens. To find the icon you want, click the Look In drop-down menu, browse through the drives and folders on your computer, and then double-click the name of a suitable icon.
6. Click the OK button.
7. You are returned to the original window. Click the Apply button.
8. Click the OK button.

Unfortunately, there isn't a simple way to restore the original icon for a desktop shortcut. Instead, it's quicker to create a new shortcut. For more information on that topic, please refer to Chapter 7.

To change icons for special shortcuts (like My Computer, My Documents, My Network Places, and the Recycle Bin):

1. Right-click the empty space on your desktop.
2. Select Properties.
3. The Display Properties window opens. Click the Desktop tab.
4. Click the Customize Desktop button located at the bottom of this window.
5. A new window opens. Under the Desktop Icons heading, you can add or remove the special shortcuts from your desktop by placing or clearing a checkmark from the corresponding boxes.
6. To change the icon for a special shortcut, click its name in the center window, and then click the Change Icon button (see Figure 11-4).

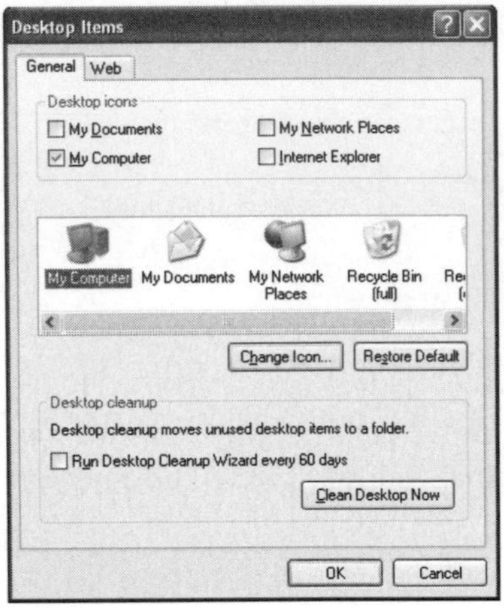

Figure 11-4

7. Another window opens. Click the Browse button.
8. Yet another window opens. To find the icon you want, click the Look In drop-down menu.
9. Browse through the drives and folders on your computer, and then double-click the name of a suitable icon.
10. Click the OK button.
11. You are returned to a previous window. Click the OK button.
12. You are returned to the Display Properties window. Click the Apply button.
13. Click the OK button.

FYI

If you feel like Windows has become boring and stale, give it an extreme visual makeover. Several companies offer software that changes the appearance of your desktop wallpaper, icons, and cursors, and wraps your folders and windows in new "skins." Two highly regarded programs are Object Desktop (`http://www.stardock.com`) and Style XP (`http://www.tgtsoft.com`).

14. To restore the original icon for a special shortcut, do the following:

   a. Right-click the empty space on your desktop.

   b. Select Properties.

   c. The Display Properties window opens. Click the Desktop tab.

   d. Click the Customize Desktop button.

   e. Click the name of the special shortcut.

   f. Click the Restore Default button.

   g. Click the OK button.

   h. You are returned to the Display Properties window. Click the Apply button.

   i. Click the OK button.

Make a Screen Capture

On occasion, you may wish to take a snapshot of your Windows desktop or the files inside a folder or window.

Here's how:

1. Do one of the following:

- To capture an image of your entire screen, press the Prt Scr key.
- To capture an image of a particular window or folder, open it, and then simultaneously press the Alt key and the Prt Scr key.

2. After the image is captured, you can edit or print it by pasting it into Microsoft's Paint program as follows:

   a. Click the Start button in the lower-left corner of Windows.

   b. Click on All Programs.

   c. Select Accessories.

   d. Select Paint.

   e. After Paint opens, click the Edit drop-down menu.

   f. Select Paste.

   g. To print the screen capture, click the File drop-down menu.

   h. Select Print.

3. Another option is to paste the screen capture into a photo-editing program like Adobe's Photoshop or Photoshop Elements, Microsoft's Digital Image or Picture It, or Ulead's PhotoImpact or Photo Express.

Change the Windows Search Character

The Windows Search Companion includes an animated cartoon character designed to make your searches more lively. If you are not fond of the character currently on display, you can switch to a different one like this:

1. Click the Start button in the lower-left corner of Windows.
2. Click on Search.
3. The Windows Search Companion opens. Use the scroll bar to locate Change preferences, and then click them.
4. Click With a Different Character.
5. An animated image of your current character appears. Below the character, click the Back or Next button to scroll through the different characters that are available.
6. To select a new character, click the OK button.

FYI

Microsoft offers numerous free downloads and enhancements for Windows XP at `http://www.microsoft.com/windowsxp/downloads`.

Paint Yourself into a Corner

If you need a digital painter that is more powerful than the no-frills Windows Paint program, consider purchasing professional software. Here are two popular titles (in no particular order):

- Ultimate Paint (`http://www.ultimatepaint.com`)
- Paint Shop Pro (`http://www.corel.com`)

View Slide Shows of Your Digital Photos

Add some pizzazz to your collection of digital photos by viewing them as a slide show. Follow these steps:

Note

This feature is available only in folders that use a "picture template" (such as My Pictures or a folder you have customized).

1. Double-click a folder containing digital pictures or photos, such as the My Pictures folder.
2. In the left window pane, look for the Picture Tasks heading. If it is there, then proceed to Step 3. If you don't see this heading, then you must apply a picture template to your folder as follows:
   a. Exit the folder by clicking the X button in the upper-right corner.
   b. Right-click the folder and select Properties.

c. A window opens. Click the Customize tab.

d. At the top of the window, under What Kind of Folder Do You Want, click the drop-down menu and select Pictures.

e. Beneath this drop-down menu, put a checkmark in the Also Apply This Template to All Subfolders box.

f. Click the Apply button.

g. Click the OK button.

h. Open the folder by double-clicking it.

3. Below Picture Tasks, click View As a Slide Show (see Figure 11-5). If you don't see this option, then you must expand the Picture Tasks category by clicking the small downward-pointing arrow.

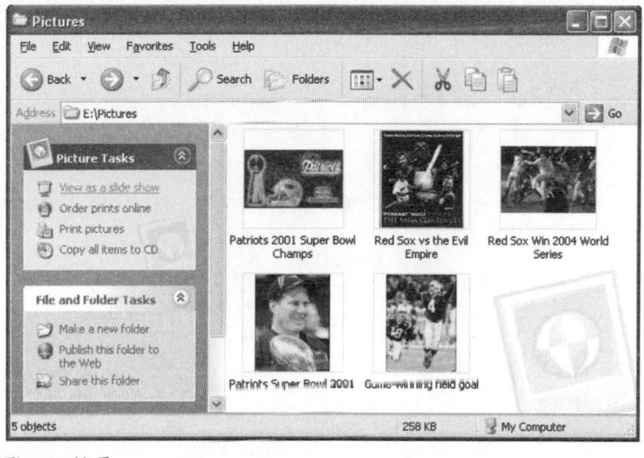

Figure 11-5

4. The slide show begins. To exit it, press the Esc key.

Disable System Sounds

By default, Windows XP plays music clips or sound effects when you do certain activities such as entering/exiting Windows and emptying the Recycle Bin. If these sounds irritate you, they can be turned off entirely. Here's how:

1. Click the Start button in the lower-left corner of Windows.
2. Click the Control Panel. (If you don't see this option, your Start menu is in classic mode. In that case, click Settings, and then select the Control Panel.)
3. If the Control Panel is in category view, click the Sounds, Speech, and Audio Devices category, and then click the Sounds and Audio Devices icon. If the Control Panel is in classic view, simply double-click the Sounds and Audio Devices icon.
4. A window opens. Click the Sounds tab.

5. To completely disable all sounds in Windows, click the Sound Scheme drop-down menu, and then select No Sounds (see Figure 11-6).

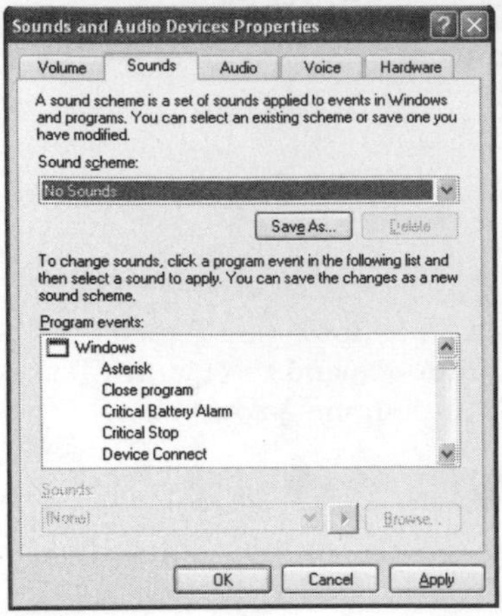

Figure 11-6

6. A message appears, asking whether or not you want to save your current sound scheme. Click the Yes button.
7. A window opens. Type a name for your current scheme, and then click the OK button.
8. Click the Apply button.
9. Click the OK button.
10. To restore the sounds in Windows, do the following:
    a. Return to the Sound Scheme drop-down menu.
    b. Select the scheme you previously saved.
    c. Click the Apply button.
    d. Click the OK button.

Customize System Sounds

If you want to continue using system sounds but dislike the ones supplied by Windows XP, you can replace them with any *wav* file on your computer (these files have the extension .wav).

Download Free Wavs

Many sites on the Internet have extensive collections of wav files that can be downloaded for free, including dialogue from movies and TV shows, sound effects, music clips, and more. Here are some of the most popular locations (in no particular order):

- **Movie Sounds Central** (`http://www.moviesoundscentral.com`)

- **The Daily Wav** (`http://www.dailywav.com`)
- **Wav Source** (`http://www.wavsource.com`)
- **Reel Wavs** (`http://www.reelwavs.com`)
- **Sound America** (`http://soundamerica.com`)
- **A1 Free Sound Effects** (`http://www.a1freesoundeffects.com`)

Switch Wavs

By default, Windows XP is configured to play sound effects when you do a special activity like empty the Recycle Bin or download e-mail. To replace these sounds with different or new ones, follow these steps.

1. Click the Start button in the lower-left corner of Windows.
2. Click the Control Panel. (If you don't see this option, your Start menu is in classic mode. In that case, click Settings, and then select the Control Panel.)
3. If the Control Panel is in category view, click the Sounds, Speech, and Audio Devices category, and then click the Sounds and Audio Devices icon. If the Control Panel is in classic view, simply double-click the Sounds and Audio Devices icon.
4. A window opens. Click the Sounds tab.
5. To change the sound for a specific action or event — like emptying the Recycle Bin or exiting Windows — go to the Program Events heading.
6. Scroll down the list, and then click the name of an action or event (see Figure 11-7).

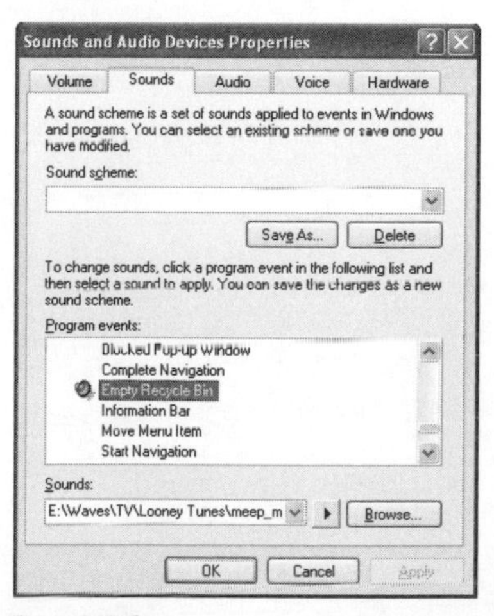

Figure 11-7

7. To select a new sound, click the Sounds drop-down menu, and then click the name of a prerecorded Windows sound.
8. To hear a preview of the sound, click the small arrow button on the right.
9. If you don't want to use one of the prerecorded Windows sounds, you can use any other wav file on your computer, like this:
   a. Click the button labeled Browse.
   b. A window opens. Click the Look In drop-down menu located at the top of this window.
   c. Browse through the drives and folders on your computer. When you find a suitable wav file, double-click its name.
   d. You are returned to the previous window, where you can preview your new sound.
10. When you have finished customizing your sound scheme, click the Apply button.
11. Click the OK button.

12

5-Minute Fixes

GROOVE TO WINDOWS MEDIA PLAYER 10

If you are a multimedia junkie, you will love the wealth of features in Microsoft's all-in-one digital entertainment center called Windows Media Player. If you don't have version 10, download it at `http://www.microsoft.com/windows/windowsmedia/mp10` (free of charge).

Note

Some of these 5-minute fixes require you to access Windows Media Player's "menu bar," which contains the drop-down menus you must click in order to change the player's settings. If the menu bar does not automatically appear at the top of your player, you can make it visible by simultaneously pressing the Ctrl key and the M key.

Do It Yourself

- Listen to Internet radio
- Create digital songs
- Purchase music online
- Edit a song's tag
- Burn custom music CDs
- Visualize your music
- Slip into a new skin
- Bulk up your music player

Listen to Internet Radio

The next time you need a little background music while using your computer, log on to the Internet. Many of your local radio stations simultaneously broadcast their free programs over the airwaves and over the Web, so you can hear them no matter where your travels take you. To listen to radiocasts in Windows Media Player 10, all you need is an Internet connection and a set of speakers and then follow these steps:

1. Turn on your computer's speakers.
2. Connect to the Internet.
3. Open Windows Media Player 10.
4. Click the Guide tab.
5. Click the Radio link (see Figure 12-1).

Figure 12-1

6. On the right side of the window, click Radio Tuner.

7. The radio tuner opens. To hear one of Microsoft's featured stations, do the following:

   a. In the center of the window, click the name of a station.

   b. A menu appears. Click Play (or in some cases Visit Website to Play).

   c. The player connects to the radio station. Depending on your Internet speed, this could take a few seconds or a few minutes. When the connection is made, music begins to play.

8. If none of the featured stations interest you, select a style of music listed on the right side of the window.

9. If you prefer a style that is not listed, then search for it, as follows:

   a. Locate the search box containing Search Keyword.

   b. Replace "Search Keyword", with a word that describes the style of music you want to hear. For example, if you want to listen to classical music, type the keyword **Classical**.

   c. Click the green arrow button or press the Enter key.

   d. A list of relevant stations appears. Click one that appeals to you.

   e. A menu appears. Click Play (or, in some cases, Visit Website to Play).

   f. The player connects to the radio station. Depending on your Internet speed, this could take a few seconds or a few minutes. When the connection is made, music begins to play.

Create Digital Songs

In years past, you had to purchase special software to convert your music CDs into digital songs like MP3s that could be played on your computer or transferred to a portable audio device. Now, Windows Media Player 10 does it all for you — for free. Try this:

1. Insert a music CD into your computer's CD or DVD drive.
2. If AutoPlay is configured to play music CDs automatically, then Windows Media Player opens (for more information on AutoPlay, please refer to Chapter 2). Otherwise, open Windows Media Player manually.
3. Click the Rip tab. A numerical list of the songs on your CD, including their duration, is displayed (see Figure 12-2).

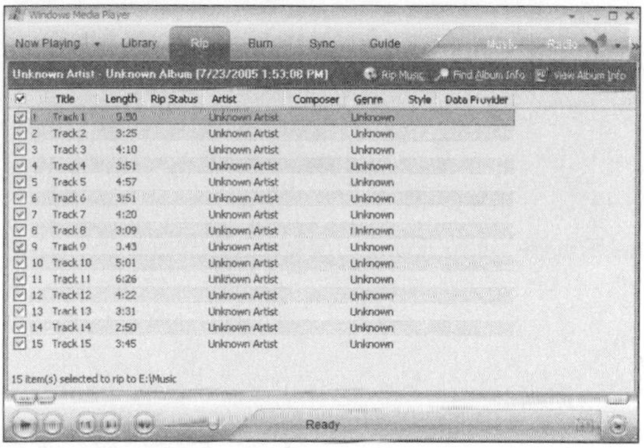

Figure 12-2

4. To have Windows Media Player automatically fill in the names of the musician, album, and songs — and even download the album's cover art — do the following:
   a. Connect to the Internet.
   b. Click the Find Album Info button located near the top-right of the player.
   c. The player connects to an online database and downloads the data for your CD.
5. Now you must tell the player what type of digital songs you want to make. Click the Tools drop-down menu.
6. Select Options.
7. A window opens. Click the Rip Music tab.
8. Under the Rip Settings heading, click the Format drop-down menu.
9. Select a style of digital song: one of Microsoft's WMA formats, or the classic MP3 format (see Figure 12-3). If you have a digital music player and want to ensure your songs play properly on it, select the MP3 format.

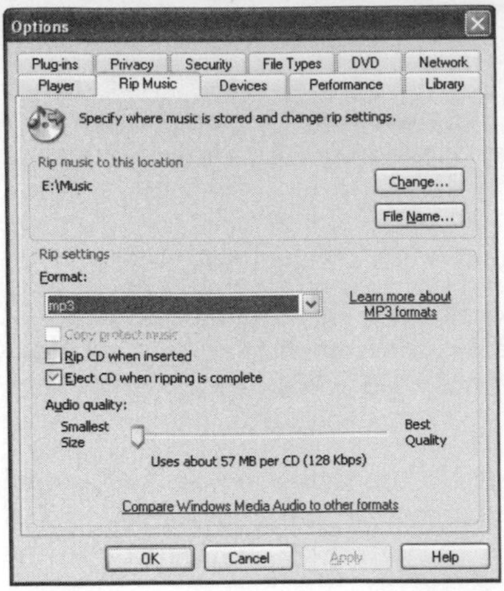

Figure 12-3

10. Use the slider bar near the bottom of the window to change the quality of your digital songs. Each time you slide the bar to the right, the songs increase in quality and file size.
11. When you are finished configuring your rip settings, click the Apply button.
12. Click the OK button.
13. You are returned to the main Rip window. Tell the player what to rip by placing checkmarks in the boxes next to the songs you want and removing checkmarks from the boxes next to the songs you don't want.
14. Click the Rip Music button located on the right side of the window.
15. A message might pop up and ask you if you want to change your rip settings. In that case, click the Keep My Current Format Settings button. Next, click the OK button.
16. The ripping and converting process begins and takes several minutes to complete (unless your computer is an older, slower model, in which case the process could take much longer). You can follow the progress by viewing the Rip Status column.

Purchase Music Online

Gone are the days when you were forced to buy an entire album just to get that one song you liked. Instead, you simply can visit a digital music store and purchase individual songs for less than a dollar a piece.

Follow these steps to purchase music through Windows Media Player 10:

1. Connect to the Internet.
2. Open Windows Media Player 10.

3. Click the View drop-down menu located at the top of the player.
4. Select Online Stores.
5. Click the name of an Internet store. This connects your player to the store's website, where you receive instructions about how to purchase songs or movies.

Note

Often this requires you to download a "plug-in" that enables your player to communicate with the store. If you are asked to download a plug-in or similar software, follow the on-screen instructions.

To purchase music through a Web browser, open a Web browser like Internet Explorer and visit one of the following sites:

- MSN Music (`http://music.msn.com`)
- Napster (`http://www.napster.com`)
- Yahoo Music Unlimited (`http://music.yahoo.com/unlimited`)
- Music Now (`http://www.musicnow.com`)
- Apple iTunes (`http://www.apple.com/itunes`)
- Rhapsody (`http://www.listen.com`)
- Wal-Mart Music Downloads (`http://musicdownloads.walmart.com`)
- eMusic (`http://www.emusic.com`)

Edit a Song's Tag

An ID3 tag is a list attached to a digital song that displays the singer's name, the title of the song and the album, and more. A great feature of Windows XP is its native support for tags, which enables you to edit them without using additional software. Here's how:

1. Locate a digital song you want to edit, such as an MP3 or WMA.
2. Right-click it and select Properties.
3. A window opens. Click the Summary tab.
4. If the center of the window displays four categories named Music, Description, Origin, and Audio, proceed to Step 5. If these categories are not available, then make them appear by clicking the Advanced button located on the right side of the window.

   On top of the four categories are Property and Value columns. Under the Property column are Artist, Album Title, Year, and so forth (see Figure 12-4).

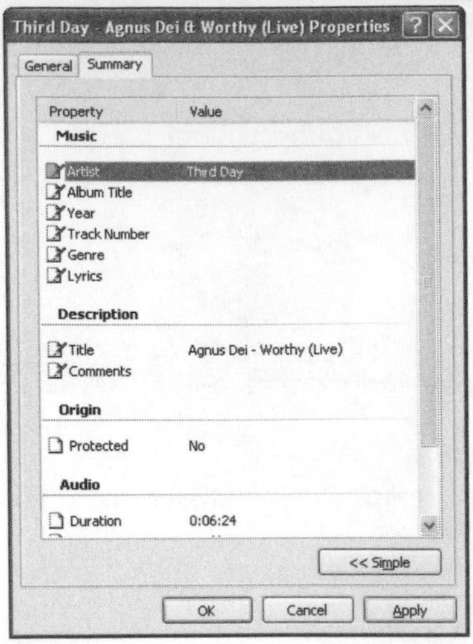

Figure 12-4

5. Underneath the Value column, there are numerous blank spaces. To fill in these blanks with information that identifies the name of the musician, the title of the album, the year the album was made, and so forth, simply click one of the blanks and type the relevant data.
6. When you finish editing the tag, click the Apply button.
7. Exit the tag by clicking the OK button.

Burn Custom Music CDs

Throughout the 1980s and most of the 1990s, the mixed tape reigned supreme. Music lovers would spend countless hours hand-picking thematically-similar songs from their favorite albums, and then would transfer them in a carefully selected order to a cassette tape. For some people, it was almost an art form. Although the emergence of recordable and rewritable CDs brought a swift end to the mixed tape, its spirit lives on in the form of custom music CDs. Follow these steps to create a custom CD:

1. Insert a recordable CD into your computer's CD or DVD drive.
2. Locate a folder containing digital songs you want to burn to the CD.
3. Hold down the Ctrl key on your keyboard while single-clicking the name of each song you want to include. This highlights all of the selected songs.
4. On the left side of the folder, look for the Music Tasks heading. Below it, click Copy to Audio CD (see Figure 12-5).
5. Windows Media Player opens. For the next few minutes, it loads your selected songs into its burning program. You will be unable to use the player during this time. When the loading process is finished, click the Burn tab.

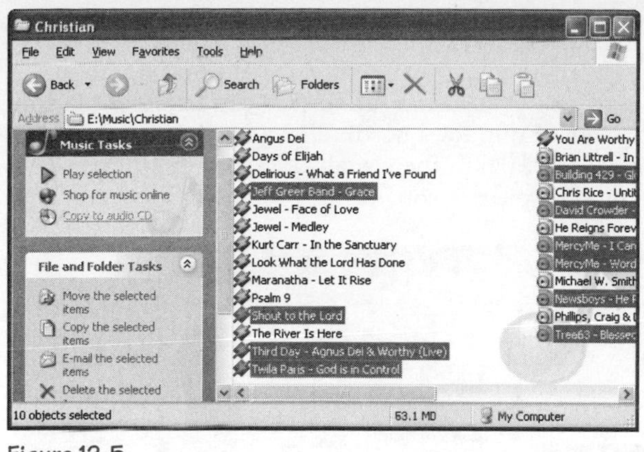

Figure 12-5

6. In the Burn window, the names of the songs you chose in the previous step are displayed. Any song that has a checkmark next to it will be burned to your CD. To prevent a song from being burned, remove the checkmark from its box.

7. To change the order in which the songs are burned to your CD, highlight a particular song by clicking it once (if you accidentally double-click the song, it begins to play). When the song is highlighted, drag it higher or lower on the burn list and drop it into a new position. Repeat this process until all of the songs are in the exact order you desire.

8. When you are ready to create your CD, click the Start Burn button located near the upper-left corner of this window.

9. The burning process begins. Depending on the speed of your CD or DVD burner, this could take between 5 and 30 minutes.

Visualize Your Music

Like most digital music software, Windows Media Player 10 enables you to "see" your songs by displaying colorful lights and images that swirl, pulse, and dance to the beat of the music. Only one word can describe this far-out feature: *groovy*.

Follow these steps to add visualizations to your music:

1. Locate a digital song you want to play, and then right-click it and select Play with Media Player.

2. Windows Media Player opens, and within a few seconds it begins to play your song.

3. Click the View drop-down menu.

4. Select Visualizations.

5. Select one of the visualization categories, such as Ambience, Particle, or Musical Colors.

6. Click the name of a specific visualization (see Figure 12-6). It appears in the main window of Windows Media Player and pulsates to the beat of your song. Try each of the visualizations in the numerous categories to find one that pleases you.

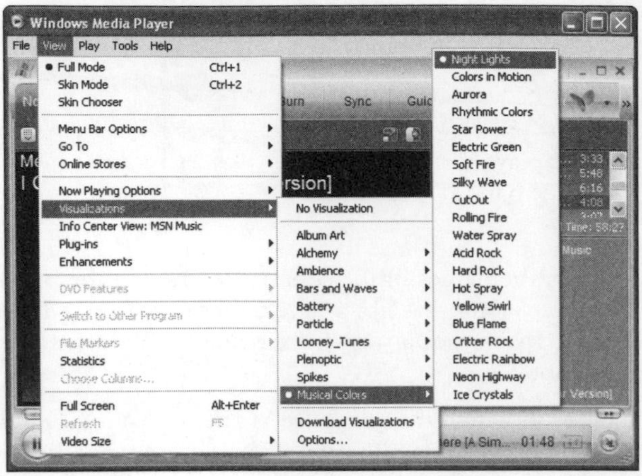

Figure 12-6

7. If you find the visualizations to be distracting, you can disable them, like this:

   a. Click the View drop-down menu.

   b. Select Visualizations.

   c. Click No Visualization.

8. To download more visualizations, do the following:

   a. Connect to the Internet.

   b. Open your Web browser, and then type **http://www.wmplugins.com** to visit the Windows Media plug-in website.

   c. When the website appears, click Visualizations. An alternate method is to click the drop-down menu on the right side of the page, select Visualization, and then click the Go button next to it.

   d. Click the name of a visualization you want to download.

   e. You are taken to a separate page. Look for Download Sites, and then click the name of the website listed.

   f. You are sent to another page that explains how to download the visualization. Follow the on-screen instructions.

   g. A message or notice might appear on-screen. If so, click I Accept located near the bottom of the page.

   h. Before the download begins, you are asked if you are sure you want to download and open the file. Click the Yes button.

Slip into a New Skin

When was the last time you shed your old skin and slipped into a new one? With Windows Media Player 10, it is easy to do. In computer terms, a skin refers to the shape and appearance of a program. By changing skins, you can give Windows Media Player the ultimate extreme makeover. Follow these steps:

1. Open Windows Media Player 10.
2. Click the View drop-down menu.
3. Click Skin Chooser.
4. Your player is divided into two window panes (see Figure 12-7). The left window pane displays the names of the skins currently installed in your player. The right pane shows a preview of the skin that is currently selected. To view a different skin, click its name in the left pane.

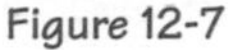
Figure 12-7

5. If you find a skin you like, apply it by double-clicking its name in the left window pane. Within seconds, your Windows Media Player sheds its old skin and puts on the new one.
6. To change skins or to restore the original Windows Media Player skin, right-click anywhere on your current skin, and then click Switch to Full Mode. The Skin Chooser reappears.
7. To download more skins, do the following:
   a. Connect to the Internet.
   b. Open your Web browser, and then type **http://www.wmplugins.com** to visit the Windows Media plug-in website.
   c. When the website appears, click Skins. An alternate method is to click the drop-down menu on the right side of the page, select Skin, and then click the Go button next to it.
   d. Click the name of a skin you want to download.
   e. You are taken to a separate page. Look for Download Sites, and then click the name of the website listed.

f. You are sent to another page that explains how to download the skin. Follow the on-screen instructions.

g. A message or notice might appear on screen. If so, click I Accept.

h. Before the download begins, you are asked if you are sure you want to download and open the file. Click the Yes button.

Bulk Up Your Music Player

If you are passionate about digital music, consider purchasing a music player that offers more ripping, converting, and CD-burning features than Windows Media Player. Here are two popular programs (in no particular order):

- Winamp (`http://www.winamp.com`)
- Musicmatch Jukebox (`http://www.musicmatch.com`)

GLOSSARY

address bar: In an Internet browser, it is the area that tells you the address of the website you are currently viewing. In a Windows folder, it is the area that tells you the path of the folder you are browsing on your hard drive. The address bar can also be used as a shortcut to jump from one website or folder to another.

Address Book: The part of Outlook Express that stores the names, numbers, and addresses of your friends, family, and other contacts.

AutoPlay: A feature built into Windows XP that can automatically perform a particular action whenever a disc is inserted into the CD/DVD drive (such as automatically playing music CDs or automatically opening digital photos in a slideshow).

back up: The process of copying your computer data onto CDs, DVDs, cassettes, thumbdrives, or secondary hard drives in order to protect that data from being damaged, destroyed, or stolen.

bookmark: A shortcut used by Internet browsers to go directly to a website.

cache (also known as the "Internet cache" or "Temporary Internet Files"): The place where Internet Explorer stores copies of the images, sounds, and other information related to the websites you have visited recently.

cookie: A small text file that stores information about the websites you have visited and the things you did on those sites.

CPU (also known as the "processor"): The heart of your computer. It follows and carries out the instructions given by your programs.

defragment: The process of rearranging and reorganizing the software and files on your hard drive to make your computer faster and more efficient.

drivers: Small pieces of software that tell your computer how it should "talk" to devices like video cards, sound cards, game pads, and so on.

encryption: The process of transforming your data into a secret code that can be viewed only by people with the correct password. With the crime of identity theft growing worse each year, encryption has become a vital part of protecting your computer from high-tech criminals.

Favicon: A small picture displayed alongside a website's address in your Internet browser's address bar.

Favorite: Another name for an Internet bookmark.

firewall: A piece of hardware or software that hides your computer from the watchful eyes of online criminals, filters the data that enters your computer, controls Internet cookies, and warns you when sinister spyware programs try to transmit data about you over the Web.

icon: A small picture used to identify folders or programs on your computer.

instant message: A simple text message sent from one person to another via special programs (like MSN Messenger, AOL Instant Messenger, Yahoo Messenger, and so on).

Messenger: A service in Windows XP that has been found to be a security hazard. Do not confuse it with the similarly named Windows Messenger, which is an instant-messaging program.

modem (cable or DSL): A device used to provide a computer with high-speed Internet access offered by a local cable company or phone company.

MP3: A type of digital song.

Notepad: A simple Windows XP program that is used to write plain-text notes or similar documents.

Outlook Express: A free program built into Windows XP that can send and receive e-mail.

Phishing: Pronounced "fishing," this Internet scam tricks people into revealing their private, personal information (like credit-card numbers and passwords).

pop-up: An Internet advertisement that suddenly appears in the middle of your computer screen while browsing a website. Some pop-ups can be carriers of spyware or other digital threats.

PowerToys: Free programs from Microsoft designed to enhance the existing features of Windows XP or add new functionality. You can download any or all PowerToys at `http://www.microsoft.com/windowsxp/downloads/powertoys/xppowertoys.mspx`.

Quick Launch Toolbar: A feature of Windows XP that enables you to access shortcuts to your favorite programs or folders.

QuickTime: A program offered by Apple to play multimedia files that have the .qt or .mov extensions (as well as other non-Apple formats).

RAM (also known as "memory"): The hardware inside your computer that temporarily stores information related to the files and programs that are being used.

Regedit: The command used to access the Windows Registry.

Registry: The inner workings of Windows. Tweaking or editing certain aspects of the Registry can change Windows' features and sometimes improve performance. Registry edits should be performed with caution, because changing the wrong part could corrupt or damage Windows to the point that it becomes unusable.

router: A device used to connect computers for the purpose of sharing files and/or an Internet connection. Many routers also have a firewall built into them to protect against Internet attacks.

spyware: A general term describing dangerous programs that sneak into your computer by tricking you into installing them or by hiding in other programs you install.

Status Bar: A feature of Windows' folders or Internet Explorer that provides extra details about the files, folders, or websites you are viewing.

System Restore: The feature of Windows XP that allows you to "go back in time" to a point when your computer was working properly.

Theme (also known as a "suite"): A collection of wallpaper, icons, cursors, and sounds that are centered around a common idea, place, movie, TV show, sports team, or other topic.

virus: A small program that is injected into your computer when you open or run an infected file. A virus can cause your computer to crash, freeze, or run slowly, and some viruses can even damage or delete your computer data.

wav: A digital audio clip.

Windows Media Player: A free program built into Windows XP that plays many different types of multimedia files.

Windows Messenger: A free program built into Windows XP that can send and receive instant messages. Do not confuse it with a security hazard in Windows known simply as Messenger.

WMA: A type of digital song.

Word: Microsoft's popular word-processing program. It does not come with Windows XP and must be purchased separately.

WordPad: A very basic word-processing program that comes free with Windows.

worm: A program that infects a computer either by slipping into a PC that hasn't been updated with the latest security patches for Windows or by being launched when an infected e-mail attachment is opened or run. In some cases, all you have to do to become infected is to access the Internet with a computer that lacks the latest Windows security patches.

INDEX

SYMBOLS

A

B

E

F

J

K

Continued

W

Y

Z